Helping Children with Mathematics

◆

Grades 3-5

James Riley

Marge Eberts

Peggy Gisler

Illustrated by **Amy O'Brien Krupp**

Dedication

To Patty White, who loves all creatures great and small, and to Rebel the horse, Scobey the dog, Swarte the cat, and Hooter the owl.

Acknowledgments

The authors acknowledge the special help of Martha Eberts in the writing of this book.

GoodYearBooks

are available for most basic curriculum subjects plus many enrichment areas. For more GoodYearBooks, contact your local bookstore or educational dealer. For a complete catalog with information about other GoodYearBooks, please write:

GoodYearBooks
ScottForesman
1900 East Lake Avenue
Glenview, IL 60025

Book design by Amy O'Brien Krupp.

Copyright © 1996 James Riley, Marge Eberts, and Peggy Gisler.
All Rights Reserved.
Printed in the United States of America.

ISBN 0-673-36155-1

1 2 3 4 5 6 7 8 9 - MH - 03 02 01 00 99 98 97 96 95

Contents

Chapter 1: **Addition and Subtraction of Whole Numbers** 17

Chapter 2: **Multiplication and Division of Whole Numbers** 35

From *Helpirg Children with Mathematics, Grades 3–5*, published by GoodYearBooks. Copyright © 1996 James Riley, Marge Eberts, and Peggy Gisler.

Chapter 3: **Fractions, Decimals, and Percents**   69

From *Helping Children with Mathematics, Grades 3–5*, published by GoodYearBooks. Copyright © 1996 James Riley, Marge Eberts, and Peggy Gisler.

Chapter 4: **Managing Information** 87

Chapter 5: **Geometry and Measurement** 101

From *Helping Children with Mathematics, Grades 3–5*, published by GoodYearBooks. Copyright © 1996 James Riley, Marge Eberts, and Peggy Gisler.

Appendix 125

An Introduction for Parents

I t's surprising to many parents to discover that the mathematics their children study in the third, fourth, and fifth grades is taught in different ways from when they went to school. Remember the days you spent adding long columns of three- and four-digit numbers and all the time it took to complete multiplication exercises like 2,374 x 489? Calculators and computers have freed children from this computational drudgery, and they are using this time to study new topics in geometry, probability, and statistics.

No longer are elementary school children just memorizing rules and doing rote drills. The emphasis today is on having children manipulate hands-on materials in such ways that they can figure out relationships and develop an understanding of mathematical concepts.

How Children Learn Math

Children learn about the properties of a cube by manipulating a block and noticing that it has 6 faces, 12 edges, and 8 vertices. They learn what place value is by grouping and regrouping single objects, such as beans into groups of ones, tens, and hundreds and figuring out that each group is ten times the size of the previous group. Mathematical concepts are relationships, and children in elementary school learn these concepts through manipulating hands-on materials until they "see" these relationships in their minds. Parents can help their children think about concepts by encouraging them to talk about what they are doing when using the materials.

Children must also learn mathematical procedures—the step-by-step acts needed to complete tasks such as finding the product of 38 x 45. Procedures can be mastered through rote learning. However, they will be learned best when children can make connections between the procedures and their underlying concepts.

How This Book Can Help You

Helping Children with Mathematics includes 71 activities which cover many of the basic mathematical concepts your children will encounter in the third, fourth, and fifth grades. You will find activities on familiar topics such as basic multiplication facts, division, and adding fractions, as well as activities that will help your children grasp the new ideas now being taught in elementary school mathematics programs, such as plane and solid geometry, graph theory, probability, and statistics. By helping your children learn these concepts, you are giving them a sound foundation for mathematics learning in elementary school and beyond.

You and your children will enjoy working through the activities in this book because they emphasize hands-on learning. This is the same approach that the National Council of Teachers of Mathematics advises teachers to use in the classroom. Through this approach, children first learn concepts and then the procedures that grow out of these concepts. For example, they first develop the idea of multiplication as repeated sets and then use this concept to learn basic multiplication "facts," such as $3 \times 4 = 12$.

Almost every activity in this book uses objects that your children can touch and move so that learning becomes less abstract and more concrete. You will find most of the materials needed for these activities right in your own home or in the insert and appendix sections of the book. You will need to purchase only a few inexpensive items.

🚫 **Warning:** Because many of the objects used in the activities are small, such as beans, or can cause injury, such as scissors, you must supervise their use.

Even if you feel your own elementary school mathematics is rusty, you'll be able to understand the instructions for the activities, helping you feel more comfortable teaching mathematical concepts to your elementary school children. Each activity includes:

◆ Activity number and title
◆ Recommended age level
◆ List of necessary materials
◆ Step-by-step-instructions on how to do the activity

Some activities also include suggestions for additional ways to perform the activity. Many include a comments section, which provides further explanation of the activity.

Although the book is organized in such a way that the concepts build on each other, there is no need to do these activities in the order presented. Begin using this book with your eight-year-old; he or she is ready to handle it. With older children, work through the entire range of topics, or select topics that are giving them trouble.

Overall, *Helping Children with Mathematics* shows you how to take an active part in helping your child learn mathematics, giving you appropriate activities for your child's age and needs. You will be giving your child the solid mathematical foundation he or she needs for future success in mathematics, and, at the same time, the two of you will enjoy working together on this new hands-on approach.

From *Helping Children with Mathematics, Grades 3–5*, published by GoodYearBooks. Copyright © 1996 James Riley, Marge Eberts, and Peggy Gisler.

An Introduction for Teachers

The *National Council of Teachers of Mathematics Curriculum and Evaluation Standards for Elementary School Mathematics,* published in 1989, tells us that the best way for children to learn mathematical concepts and retain what they have learned is through hands-on experiences. In addition, before children can learn procedures they must have a grasp of the concepts that underlie those procedures.

The 71 activities in *Helping Children with Mathematics* are designed and organized to teach and reinforce many of the basic mathematical concepts that children should learn in the third, fourth, and fifth grades, as prescribed by the NCTM Standards. However, as educators, we know that activities are not effective simply because they are developmentally appropriate. They must also present interesting, enjoyable, and positive experiences for children. You will find that the activities in this book accomplish these objectives.

◆ Because learning mathematics should not be boring, the activities in this book challenge children to use their imagination and creativity in finding solutions to problems and developing an understanding of basic mathematical concepts.

◆ Children will not encounter failure in doing the activities; each activity presents strategies for finding correct solutions.

◆ The mathematics activities in this book are integrated with other curriculum areas to provide children with a real-life environment in learning mathematics. These interrelated experiences help children retain what they have learned.

Depending on what grade or grades you teach, you can use this book in a number of different ways.

◆ The book can be used in third-, fourth-, and fifth-grade classrooms to provide individual students or an entire class with valuable hands-on mathematics experiences, beyond the textbook.

◆ All teachers can use the activities in this book to involve parents effectively in their children's efforts to learn mathematics. Parents frequently ask teachers for assistance when they do not know how to help their children with mathematics. This book is a resource of activities that teachers can pass on to parents.

◆ The book can be a source of homework assignments since the activities were designed to be completed in the home. The activities are nonroutine and more enjoyable and thought-provoking than many "ditto sheets" used for homework assignments.

◆ In both remedial and gifted mathematics classes, the hands-on activities in this book can be used to help children master basic mathematics concepts. In addition, aides can use this book in the classroom for both remedial and enrichment work with children.

◆ The book could serve as a textbook for a parent/teacher workshop for parents who wish to prepare themselves to help their children with mathematics at home.

Finally, you will already have most of the materials needed to complete the activities, or you will find them in this book's insert or appendix. You should only need to purchase a few inexpensive items.

Helping Children with Mathematics is designed to give parents a solid way to help their children learn many of the basic mathematical concepts that children should master by the end of the fifth grade. The activities introduce concepts before procedures and involve children in hands-on mathematics experiences. You can suggest activities to parents, confident that the activities follow NCTM Standards.

How to Use This Book

Organization

Helping Children with
Mathematics is divided
into five chapters. Chapters
1, 2, and 3 deal with numbers and computational
skills as children work with
addition, subtraction, multiplication, division, fractions,
decimals, and percents.
Chapter 4, "Managing
Information," introduces
some topics in graphing,
probability, and statistics. The final chapter, "Geometry and
Measurement," provides a limited, but highly imaginative, approach
to this broad topic by relating the mathematics to real-life applica-
tions. The book is organized so that each chapter is broken down into
subsequent topics, presented in a progressive order that corresponds
to the standards of the National Council of Teachers of Mathematics
for children in grades three, four, and five.

Every chapter begins with an explanation that tells you what
children will learn in the chapter. Similarly, each section within a
chapter includes a thorough explanation of the mathematical background of the section's concept as well as the purpose of the activities.

Individual activities deal with the development of mathematical
concepts and/or rules and procedures. You will find that every activity
has a number, a title, a recommended age level, a list of materials
needed, and instructions for the activity. Some activities have a
"Further Work" section suggesting additional ways to do the activity.
Many include a "Comments" section with additional explanation of
the activity. The book includes a number of activities for calculators.
Make sure your child has a four-function calculator with an automatic
constant function.

Using the Book

In general, you don't have to start at the beginning of the book
and work through every activity in sequence. You can start on any
topic, and children will enjoy moving from one topic to another. They
can move from a multiplication activity to a geometry activity.

However, the activities within each section should be taken in order because the concepts build on each other. For example, the games that reinforce the learning of basic multiplication facts should not be played until the previous activities presenting the facts have been mastered.

If you follow the age guidelines, you can be fairly certain that your children will have the background necessary for the activity. If your child seems to have difficulty with an activity at his or her age level, it may be necessary to begin at a younger age level or work with activities in *Helping Your Child with Mathematics,* the first book in this series. Going to other activities does not mean that your child is behind in mathematics. It simply means that your child has not yet had the experiences needed to grasp the ideas required to complete the activity.

Most activities will take 30 minutes or less to complete; however, some of the activities are extended over a period of days. Even the longer activities can be broken up into short daily sessions. You will be amazed at how much your children learn in 30-minute sessions. Short sessions three or four times a week accomplish far more than a weekly hour-long session. Of course, if your child becomes engrossed in an activity and wishes to continue, there is no reason to stop, but never force a child to continue an activity until it is done without error.

Extra Help

For extra help in doing the activities, turn to the following:

◆ **Glossary:** We've included a glossary of mathematical terms that may be unfamiliar to parents, on page 8. You'll also find each term defined the first time it is used in the book.

◆ **Cross-Curriculum Areas Index:** This index lists content areas (other than mathematics) that are included in each activity. Both parents and teachers can see how each activity helps children develop interrelated skills.

◆ **Appendix:** Many of the materials needed to complete the activities are included in the appendix. These materials can easily be prepared for use in the activities.

Coordinating the Activities with Classroom Work

Consult the table of contents to find the activities that are related to what your child is studying in the classroom. In addition, ask your child's classroom teacher to coordinate school and home activities, depending on the individual needs of your child.

From *Helping Children with Mathematics, Grades 3–5,* published by GoodYearBooks. Copyright © 1996 James Riley, Marge Eberts, and Peggy Gisler.

Pointing Out Mistakes

You should not have to point out mistakes, because most of the activities are designed in such a way that they are self-correcting. It is a good idea for children to determine the correctness of their work. Even in those activities where correctness is not obvious, the child can look back at previous activities for help with the current activity.

Repeating Activities

Activities can be repeated many times. Some activities will need to be repeated to help children grasp the concepts. Some activities include suggestions for performing them in different ways.

Evaluation

The activities are meant to be enjoyed, so formal evaluation is not a part of this program. Learning will take place naturally, and you will become aware of your children's progress as you move through the activities in the book.

Materials

We've provided most of the materials needed for the activities in the appendix and insert sections. Other materials like scissors, rulers, glue, pencils, and paper are usually found in the home. Craft sticks are available at teacher supply and toy stores.

Glossary

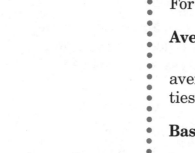

Addend

A number which is to be added to another number. For example, in the mathematical sentence 89 + 32 = 121, 89 and 32 are addends.

Algorithm

Step-by-step rules for completing a mathematics computation.

Area

The measure of the surface inside a shape.

Associative Property of Multiplication

The way in which factors are grouped does not affect the product. For example, 2 x (4 x 7) = (2 x 4) x 7.

Average

This is an everyday term for the math term *mean*. To obtain the average of a group of numbers (quantities), add the group of quantities together. Then divide by the number of quantities.

Basic Facts

The addition, subtraction, and multiplication facts that children should commit to memory. For example, the basic facts for multiplication are the products of 0 x 0 through 9 x 9.

Central Angle of a Circle

An angle formed by any two radii of a circle.

Circumference

The distance around a circle.

Commutative Property of Multiplication

The order in which two factors are multiplied does not affect the product. For example, 3 x 7 = 7 x 3.

Composite Number

A number that has more than two factors. For example, 10 is a composite number, because it has 4 factors, 1, 2, 5, and 10. 11 is not a composite number, because it has only 2 factors, itself and 1.

From *Helping Children with Mathematics, Grades 3–5*, published by GoodYearBooks. Copyright © 1996 James Riley, Marge Eberts, and Peggy Gisler.

Cube

A solid that has six squares as its faces.

Decimal

A number that is written using place value and a decimal point, such as 12.78 or 0.29.

Denominator

The bottom number of a fraction. It represents the total number of parts of the whole. In the fraction 2/3, 3 is the denominator.

Difference

The answer to a subtraction problem. For example, in the problem 57 - 43 = 14, 14 is the difference.

Digit

A single figure used to represent a numerical value. For example, the number 235 contains the digits 2, 3, and 5.

Distributive Property

A multiplication fact can be expressed as the sum of two previously learned facts, for example, $3 \times 7 = 3 \times (3 + 4) = (3 \times 3) + (3 \times 4) = 9 + 12 = 21$.

Divisor

A number that divides another number. For example, in the mathematical sentence $8 \div 4 = 2$, the divisor is 4.

Dodecahedron

A solid that has 12 regular pentagons as its faces.

Equation

A mathematical sentence using the = sign. For example, $8 \div 4 = 2$ and $3 + 5 = 4 \times 2$ are equations.

Equivalent Fractions

Different fractions that represent the same number. For example, 1/2 = 2/4 = 3/6.

Factor

A number which is to be multiplied by another number. For example, in the mathematical sentence $7 \times 8 = 56$, 7 and 8 are factors.

Graphing

The presentation of information in a pictorial manner.

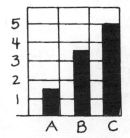

Hypotenuse

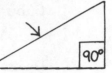

The side opposite the right angle of a right triangle.

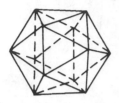

Icosahedron

A solid that has 20 regular triangles as its faces.

Improper Fraction

A fraction that represents a mixed number such as 11/4 or a whole number such as 4/1.

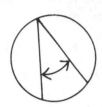

Inscribed Angle of a Circle

An angle formed by any two chords in a circle.

Mean

Also called the "average" of a group of numbers. To obtain the mean of a group of numbers (quantities), add the group of quantities together. Then divide by the number of quantities. For example, the mean of 4, 5, 6, 7, and 8 is $4 + 5 + 6 + 7 + 8 = 30 \div 5 = 6$.

Median

The median is the middle number in a group of numbers listed in order from smallest to largest. If the group contains an even number of numbers, then the median is the average of the two middle numbers. For example, the median of 2, 4, 6, 8, and 10 is 6, while the median of 2, 4, 6, 8, 10, and 12 is 7.

Mixed Number

A number represented by a whole number and a fraction, such as 2 3/4.

Mode

The most frequent outcome. It is the number that occurs most frequently in a given set of numbers. For example, the mode of 3, 5, 5, and 7 is 5.

Model

The hands-on materials, such as blocks, counters, and flash cards that are used to demonstrate a concept. When you use these materials to represent a concept, you "model" the concept.

Numerator

The top number of a fraction. It represents the number of equal parts being considered. In the fraction 2/3, 2 is the numerator.

Octahedron

A solid that has 8 triangles as its faces.

From *Helping Children with Mathematics, Grades 3–5*, published by GoodYearBooks. Copyright © 1996 James Riley, Marge Eberts, and Peggy Gisler.

Operation

Any mathematical process such as addition, subtraction, multiplication, or division.

Ordered Pair

A number pair used to locate a point in a grid, such as (4,6) in which 4 is the first number and 6 is the second number. The ordered pair (4,6) describes a different point on the grid than (6,4) does.

Parallelogram

A four-sided figure with its opposite sides parallel.

Pentagon

A five-sided figure.

Percent

A term indicating "hundredths" or "out of every 100." Often the symbol % is used to stand for the word "percent." For example, 25% means 25 out of every 100, or 25 percent.

Place Value

A number system in which the value of a digit depends upon its place within the entire numeral. For example, in the numeral 376, the 3 in the third place to the right represents 3 hundreds, the seven in the second place to the right represents 7 tens, and the 6 at the far right represents 6 ones.

Polygon

A closed figure, the sides or edges of which are line segments.

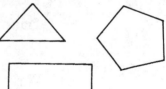

Polyhedron

A geometric solid with polygonal faces.

Probability

The mathematics of prediction. When there is more than one possible outcome of an event, probability tells you the likelihood that a certain outcome will occur. Probability is expressed as a number from 0 to 1, with 0 indicating no chance of its occurrence and 1 indicating certainty.

Product

The result of the multiplication of two factors. For example, in the mathematical sentence 7 x 8 = 56, the product is 56.

Quadrilateral

A four-sided figure.

Quotient

The answer to a division problem. For example, in the mathematical sentence 8 ÷ 2 = 4, the quotient is 4.

Range

The difference between the greatest number and least number in a set of numbers.

Statistics

The science of assembling, classifying, and analyzing facts or data.

Sum

The answer to an addition problem. For example, in the mathematical sentence 58 + 20 = 78, the sum is 78.

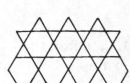

Tessellation

The covering of a flat surface with geometric shapes in a repeating pattern with no gaps or overlaps.

Tetrahedron

A solid that has four triangles as its faces.

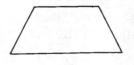

Trapezoid

A four-sided figure with two parallel sides.

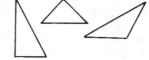

Triangle

A three-sided figure.

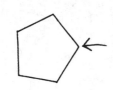

Vertex

The point of intersection of the edges of a polygon or a polyhedron.

Volume

The amount of space inside an object; the number of cubic unit measures that it will take to fill the object.

From *Helping Children with Mathematics, Grades 3–5*, published by GoodYearBooks. Copyright © 1996 James Riley, Marge Eberts, and Peggy Gisler.

Cross-Curriculum Areas Index

Research shows that children learn successfully when learning takes place in an environment that draws skills and concepts from more than one curriculum area. The mathematics activities in this book are integrated with concepts and materials from other childhood curriculum areas to provide children with a real-life environment in which to learn mathematics. The following table shows the other areas that each activity develops.

		small motor	language	art	social skills	science	imagination and creativity
Place Value Activity 1	Bean Sticks	◆		◆			
Place Value Activity 2	Base Blocks	◆		◆			
Place Value Activity 3	Sticks for Trading	◆		◆			
Place Value Activity 4	Heavy Lifters	◆	◆				
Addition Activity 1	Trading Up	◆			◆		
Addition Activity 2	Bean Stick Addition	◆	◆				
Addition Activity 3	Trading Stick Addition	◆					
Addition Activity 4	Drop That Ten	◆	◆				◆
Addition Activity 5	It's All in Your Mind						◆
Subtraction Activity 1	Trading Down	◆			◆		
Subtraction Activity 2	Bean Stick Subtraction	◆	◆				
Subtraction Activity 3	Trading Stick Subtraction	◆					
Basic Multiplication Activity 1	Making Multiplication Flash Cards	◆		◆			
Region I Activity 1	Repeated Addition	◆	◆				
Region I Activity 2	Arrays of Blocks	◆					
Region I Activity 3	The Array Lattice	◆					
Region I Activity 4	The Tic-Tac Game	◆				◆	
Region II Activity 1	Distributive Property Modeled	◆	◆				
Region II Activity 2	Distributive Property Pictured	◆		◆			

From *Helping Children with Mathematics, Grades 3–5*, published by GoodYearBooks. Copyright © 1996 James Riley, Marge Eberts, and Peggy Gisler.

Cross-Curriculum Areas Index, cont.

		small motor	language	art	social skills	science	imagination and creativity
Region II Activity 3	The Distributive Property as Procedure	◆	◆				
Region III Activity 1	The Commutative Property	◆					
Region IV Activity 1	The Magic Nines	◆	◆				◆
Region IV Activity 2	The Associative Property	◆	◆				
All Regions Activity 1	The Advanced Tic-Tac Game	◆			◆		
All Regions Activity 2	Play Multiplication Scramble	◆			◆		◆
All Regions Activity 3	Play Multipaths	◆	◆		◆		◆
All Regions Activity 4	Factor Codes	◆	◆		◆		
Multiplication Activity 1	Bean Stick Multiplication	◆					
Multiplication Activity 2	Base Blocks	◆					
Division Activity 1	Give Everyone the Same	◆	◆				
Division Activity 2	Everyone Shares Fairly	◆	◆				
Division Activity 3	Play Divingo	◆			◆		◆
Division Activity 4	Play Cross Out	◆	◆		◆		◆
Division Activity 5	Trading in for Long Division	◆					
Division Activity 6	Play High Quotient	◆		◆	◆		◆
All Operations Activity 1	Mrs. Gaylord's Fifth-Grade Game						◆
All Operations Activity 2	Challenge Solitaire	◆					◆
Fraction Concept Activity 1	Making Fraction Pieces	◆		◆			◆
Fraction Concept Activity 2	Fraction Trains	◆	◆				◆
Fraction Concept Activity 3	Equivalent Fraction Trains	◆					◆
Fraction Concept Activity 4	Fraction Concentration	◆			◆		◆
Fraction Concept Activity 5	Mixing Fractions	◆					
Fraction Activity 1	Addition of Fractions with Like Denominators	◆	◆				◆
Fraction Activity 2	Subtraction of Fractions with Like Denominators	◆	◆				◆
Fraction Activity 3	Addition of Fractions with Unlike Denominators	◆	◆				◆
Fraction Activity 4	Subtraction of Fractions with Unlike Denominators	◆	◆				◆
Fraction Multiplication Activity 1	Whole Number Times a Fraction	◆					◆
Fraction Multiplication Activity 2	Fraction Piece Multiplication	◆		◆			◆

From *Helping Children with Mathematics, Grades 3–5*, published by GoodYearBooks. Copyright © 1996 James Riley, Marge Eberts, and Peggy Gisler.

Cross-Curriculum Areas Index, cont.

		small motor	language	art	social skills	science	imagination and creativity
Fraction Multiplication Activity 3	Rectangular Multiplication	◆		◆			◆
Decimal Activity 1	Money, Money, Money	◆	◆				◆
Decimal Activity 2	Use Your Calculator	◆	◆				◆
Percent Activity 1	Percents in the News	◆	◆				
Graphing Activity 1	Get a Line on Your Team	◆		◆			
Graphing Activity 2	Measure Your Cool	◆	◆			◆	
Graphing Activity 3	How's the Weather There?	◆		◆		◆	
Probability Activity 1	Differences Among Dice	◆		◆		◆	◆
Probability Activity 2	What's for Dinner, Chicken or Fish?	◆					◆
Statistics Activity 1	How Long Is a Word?	◆		◆		◆	
Statistics Activity 2	Who's Talking Now?	◆		◆	◆		
Statistics Activity 3	The A&G 5 Stock Average	◆		◆			◆
A Different Geometry Activity 1	Take a Walk Through Konigsberg	◆		◆			◆
A Different Geometry Activity 2	Have You Got It Covered?	◆	◆	◆			
A Different Geometry Activity 3	Creating Vertex Patterns	◆		◆			
Drawing, Cutting, and Folding Activity 1	Getting the Angle on Polygons	◆		◆			
Drawing, Cutting, and Folding Activity 2	Getting the Angle on Circles	◆		◆			
Drawing, Cutting, and Folding Activity 3	The Idea Pythagoras Stole	◆		◆			
Solid Geometry Activity 1	The Regular Solids	◆		◆			◆
Area Measurement Activity 1	Playing with Cards	◆				◆	
Area Measurement Activity 2	Making Secret Formulas	◆					◆
Volume Measurement Activity 1	In the Kitchen					◆	
Time Measurement Activity 1	Call Time Out	◆		◆			

From *Helping Children with Mathematics, Grades 3–5*, published by GoodYearBooks. Copyright © 1996 James Riley, Marge Eberts, and Peggy Gisler.

Addition and Subtraction of Whole Numbers

Children should have learned the basic addition and subtraction facts by the time they are in third grade. If your child is not at ease with these facts, use the activities in *Helping Your Child with Mathematics,* the first book in this series.

Once children can easily handle the basic facts, they are ready to move on to adding and subtracting numbers with two or more digits (figures used to represent numerical values). But before they learn all the necessary procedures, they must begin by understanding the concepts, especially place value, which are the foundation of the procedures. Unfortunately, children can't be shown concepts directly, but they can manipulate hands-on materials, called models, to see exactly how addition and subtraction work. The activities in this chapter concentrate on the development of the rules and procedures for adding and subtracting numbers with two or more digits.

Place Value

Prior to the fifteenth century, most Western Europeans used Roman numerals. Today, we use a number system called the Hindu-Arabic numeration system. This is a place value system, meaning that the value of a digit depends on its place within the entire numeral. The 3 in 4,532 represents 3 tens because it occupies the second place from the right in the numeral. The 3 in 4,376 means 3 hundreds because it is in the third place from the right in the numeral.

The following activities illustrate the place value concept with concrete and abstract models. The bean stick and base block activities use objects that show your child that a tens piece is actually ten times larger than a ones piece and a hundreds piece is actually ten times larger than a tens piece. The other activities use trading sticks which are a more abstract representation of numbers because their color determines their place value, not size. Because the concept of place value is so sophisticated, children in the elementary grades need to repeat these activities many times.

Place Value Activity 1

Bean Sticks

(age 8 and older)

▼

Materials

Craft sticks
Tube of glue
Bags of dried navy
  or northern beans
Cardboard

Procedure

This activity is also found in the previous book, *Helping Your Child with Mathematics.* Your child will make a set of bean sticks that will be used in further activities including addition, subtraction, multiplication, and division procedures.

Have your child count out ten beans. Then have her glue the beans in a line on a craft stick. This is called a "bean stick." When she has made ten bean sticks, glue them side-by-side onto a piece of square cardboard as illustrated on the following page. The cardboard from empty shoe or cereal boxes works fine for this. These completed boards are called "bean flats." A bean flat will contain 100 beans.

From *Helping Children with Mathematics, Grades 3–5,* published by GoodYearBooks. Copyright © 1996 James Riley, Marge Eberts, and Peggy Gisler.

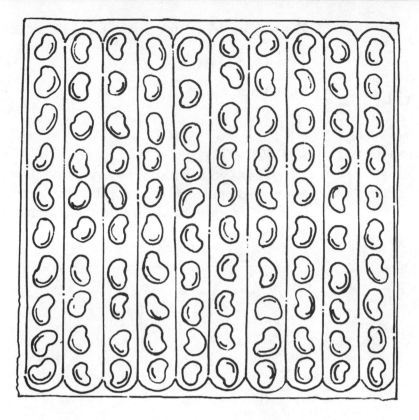

A complete set of bean sticks and bean flats should contain 10 bean flats, 30 bean sticks, and a bunch of loose beans. It will take more than one session to make a complete set.

Further Work

The bean flats, bean sticks, and loose beans will be used to represent numbers up to 1,000. For example, two bean flats, four bean sticks, and one loose bean represent 241. Lay out a number of bean flats, bean sticks, and loose beans. Ask your child what number they represent.

Reverse the process. Ask your child to use beans to show you a number such as 375. She should lay out 3 bean flats, 7 bean sticks, and 5 loose beans.

Comments

Although it is considerable work to glue so many beans on sticks, the value of this effort lies in what your child is learning. By counting out ten beans and gluing them on a stick, your child comes to realize that ten ones is the same as one ten (10 loose beans = 1 stick, or one ten). While this is obvious to adults, children need hands-on experience to acquire this important basic concept of mathematics. Furthermore, the size difference between a bean, bean stick, and bean flat allows your child to easily see the physical relationship that exists between ones, tens, and hundreds.

From *Helping Children with Mathematics, Grades 3–5*, published by GoodYearBooks. Copyright © 1996 James Riley, Marge Eberts, and Peggy Gisler.

Place Value Activity 2

Base Blocks

(age 8 and older)

Procedure

Have your child make a set of base blocks using the pattern below. The pattern shows a flat (hundreds), a long (tens), and a unit (ones). A complete set of base blocks should include 10 flats, 30 longs, and 60 units.

Materials

A set of base
blocks (see below)
Pencil and scissors
Cardboard

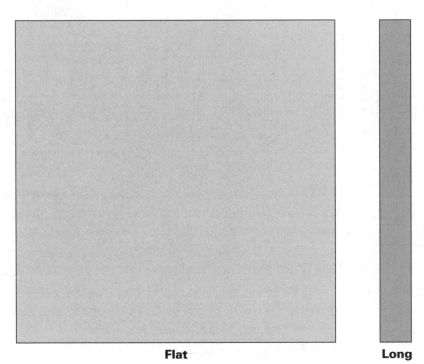

Flat

Unit

Long

Have your child explore the relationships among the base blocks. She should notice that it takes 10 longs to cover up 1 flat and that it takes 10 units to cover up 1 long.

Further Work

Rework the activities in this chapter that call for the use of bean sticks with your base blocks set to reinforce the place value concept.

Comments

Base blocks are very similar to bean sticks. Because they are proportional in size, your child can easily see that a long is ten times larger than a unit and a flat is ten times larger than a long. You can use base blocks in place of bean sticks in any activity.

From *Helping Children with Mathematics, Grades 3–5*, published by GoodYearBooks. Copyright © 1996 James Riley, Marge Eberts, and Peggy Gisler.

Place Value Activity 3

Sticks for Trading

(age 8 and older)

▼

Procedure

In this activity, your child will make a set of trading sticks and a place value mat which will be used in further activities.

Have your child color 100 craft sticks yellow, 100 blue, 100 green, and 10 red. These colored sticks are called "trading sticks."

Have your child make a place value mat from standard sheets of typing paper. Have her turn the paper on its side, and divide the paper into four equal up and down sections with a marking pen. She should color the tops of these sections starting from the left red, green, blue, and yellow. You may want to make a larger mat than this one. A place value mat is illustrated below.

Red	Green	Blue	Yellow

Trading sticks will be used to represent numbers. Reds are thousands, greens hundreds, blues tens, and yellows ones. For example, 3,476 is represented as 3 red, 4 green, 7 blue, and 6 yellow trading sticks. The place value mat will be used to show place value position according to the color code of the trading sticks. Trading sticks should be placed on the matching color code section of the place value mat.*

* The colors selected here correspond to the ones in the commercially developed mathematics program called Trading Chips® which your child may be using in her school system.

From *Helping Children with Mathematics, Grades 3–5*, published by GoodYearBooks. Copyright © 1996 James Riley, Marge Eberts, and Peggy Gisler.

Ask your child to lay out trading sticks on the place value mat to represent a number in the thousands like 4,576. She should lay out 4 red, 5 green, 7 blue, and 6 yellow trading sticks.

Reverse the process. Lay out a number of trading sticks on the place value mat like 3 red, 5 green, 2 blue, and 8 yellow trading sticks. Ask your child to tell you what number this represents. In this case, the answer should be 3,528.

Comments

Trading sticks build upon what your child has learned about place value using beans and base blocks. Unlike the other two models, the trading sticks are all the same size. The trading sticks show a more abstract representation of numbers than the bean sticks or base blocks because they are nonproportional. They differ only in color.

Place Value Activity 4

Heavy Lifters

(age 8 and older)

Procedure

This activity works with place value in the hundreds position. To handle this effectively, your child will need to make from 100 to 300 or more additional yellow trading sticks.

Place all of the yellow trading sticks into the bag. Have your child reach into the bag and take out several huge handfuls. Next, have her count the sticks one-by-one to determine how many there are, and record the number. Then, place the yellow sticks on the yellow portion of the place value mat.

Have her count out ten yellow sticks and trade them for a blue stick. Then, have her lay the blue stick on the place value mat. She is to continue trading yellow for blue sticks until no more trades are possible. Next, your child should trade ten blue sticks for one green stick, continuing until no more trades are possible.

When your child is finished trading, have her compare the number of greens, blues, and yellows with the number of hundreds, tens, and ones in her recorded count of yellow sticks.

Further Work

Place the yellow sticks in one bag and the blue sticks in another bag. Have your child take several handfuls from each bag. Lay the sticks on the place value mat in the appropriate sections. Starting with the yellow sticks, have her trade for blue sticks as above. Trading the colored sticks should continue until no more trades are possible. Have her tell you what the number of sticks is.

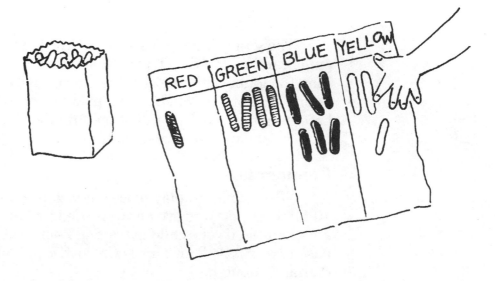

Materials

A bag
A set of trading
  sticks and a place
  value mat made in
Place Value
Activity 3
Pencil and paper

Addition of Whole Numbers

The availability of inexpensive calculators makes it unnecessary for children to become highly skilled in adding long columns of multidigit numbers. They must, however, be able to add short columns. The activities in this section begin by helping your child develop an understanding of the concept of addition of multidigit numbers. This paves the way for her to move on to paper and pencil activities and mental arithmetic exercises later in the section.

Addition Activity 1

Trading Up

(age 8 and older)

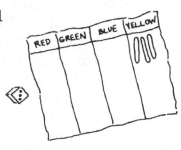

Materials

A set of trading sticks and place value mats made in Place Value Activity 3

A pair of dice

Procedure

This game can be played by two to four players. Each player will need a place value mat.

Players take turns rolling a die. The die indicates the number of yellow sticks to add to the place value mat.

Whenever a player has three yellow sticks on her mat, the three yellow sticks can be traded for one blue stick. Likewise, three blue sticks can be exchanged for one green stick, and three green sticks for one red stick. The first player to trade up to a red stick is declared the "winner."

Further Work

The game described above has the players trading 3-for-1. The game can be played by trading any amount from 2-for-1 to 10-for-1. Play the game with one of these alternative trade rates. If trades of 6-for-1 or more are made, use a pair of dice to keep the game from becoming too long. The roll of the first die should name the number of blue sticks and the second die the number of yellow sticks.

Comments

When children play place value games making trades other than 10-for-1, the players are not working in what is known as "base ten." For example if your child is trading 2-for-1 or 4-for-1, she is working in base two or base four. This is the arithmetic used by electronic digital computers.

From *Helping Children with Mathematics, Grades 3–5*, published by GoodYearBooks. Copyright © 1996 James Riley, Marge Eberts, and Peggy Gisler.

Addition Activity 2

Bean Stick Addition

(age 8 and older)

Materials

Loose beans, bean
sticks, and bean
flats (see Place
Value Activity 1)
Pencil and paper
Your child's
mathematics
textbook

Procedure

Find a page in your child's mathematics textbook that contains addition problems with three-digit addends (numbers that are being added) like 376 + 285. Have her find the sums (answers in addition) of each problem using the following procedure.

Your child should represent the three-digit addends of a problem using loose beans, bean sticks, and bean flats. The problem 376 + 285 would be represented as follows.

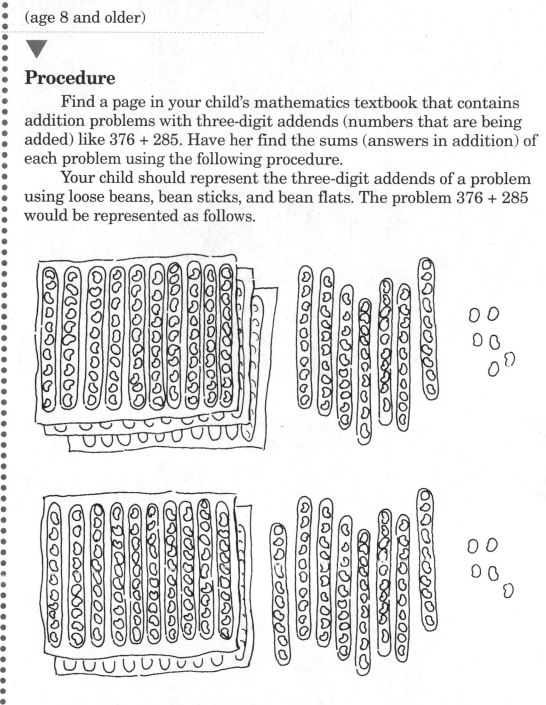

Next, have your child combine all of the loose beans and count them. If the sum of loose beans is ten or more, then the ten beans should be traded for a bean stick. Since 6 ones and 5 ones combine to make 11 ones, she can exchange 10 of the 11 beans for a bean stick. Place that bean stick above the other bean sticks as shown on the following page.

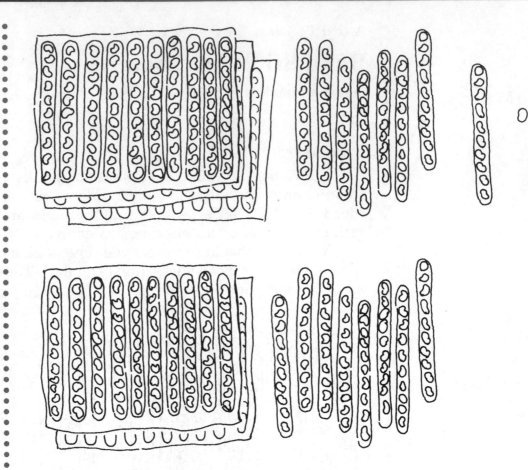

Your child should record the steps she has taken so far with pencil and paper as follows.

BEAN FLATS	BEAN STICKS	LOOSE BEANS
3	7	6
2	8	5

Now your child should combine all the bean sticks and count them. If the sum is ten bean sticks or more, then she should trade ten bean sticks for a flat of 100 beans. Since 1 traded bean stick plus 7 bean sticks plus 8 bean sticks makes 16 bean sticks, your child can exchange 10 of the 16 bean sticks for a bean flat. She should record these trades with pencil and paper. Finally, have her combine all the bean flats, count them, and record their number. When she adds 376

From *Helping Children with Mathematics, Grades 3–5*, published by GoodYearBooks. Copyright © 1996 James Riley, Marge Eberts, and Peggy Gisler.

to 285, there should be 6 bean flats, 6 bean sticks, and 1 loose bean. Her end result should look like the following:

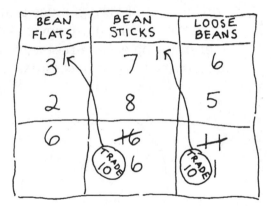

Comments

It is always a good idea to record the results of an activity with pencil and paper. Having your child record the facts helps her retain those facts. She is doing, seeing, talking, hearing, and writing. All of this aids memory and understanding.

Addition Activity 3

Trading Stick Addition

(age 8 or older)

From *Helping Children with Mathematics, Grades 3–5*, published by GoodYearBooks. Copyright © 1996 James Riley, Marge Eberts, and Peggy Gisler.

Materials

A set of trading
 sticks and a place
 value mat made in
 Place Value
 Activity 3
Pencil and paper
Your child's
 mathematics
 textbook

Procedure

Have your child use trading sticks to work through a set of three-digit addition problems from her mathematics textbook following the procedure described in Addition Activity 2.

In this activity, trading sticks are used to represent the addends instead of bean sticks. Remember that the yellow sticks are ones, blues are tens, and greens are hundreds. Also, the place value mat is used for the placement of the sticks.

Comments

The only difference between this activity and Bean Stick Addition is that here you use a more abstract representation of numbers rather than a more obvious one. If your child has gained a good understanding of the process from Bean Stick Addition, you may find this activity to be unnecessary.

Addition Activity 4

Drop That Ten

(age 8 and older)

▼

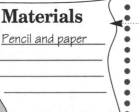

Materials

Pencil and paper

Procedure

This activity shows an easy way to find the sum of a long list of digits like the one below.

$$7 + 5 + 9 + 8 + 4 + 5 + 9 + 6$$

When children add columns of one-digit numbers, they have difficulty trying to remember the addition facts plus "dragging" the tens along. The strategy here is to drop those tens or not to carry them.

Your child will add $7 + 5$ as she has always done and get 12. Instead of trying to add $12 + 9$, she will put a line through the 5 indicating that she has not carried the ten. She must just remember the 2. Then she will add $2 + 9$ and get 11. She draws a line through the 9 to show that she dropped the ten. Now she must just remember the 1. Continue this way through all the numbers. At the end, she will write the 3 down in the ones column like this:

$$7 + \cancel{5} + \cancel{9} + 8 + \cancel{4} + 5 + \cancel{9} + \cancel{6} = 3$$

Have your child count all the lines that she has drawn through the numbers. Since she has drawn five lines, she carried 5 tens and will write 5 down in the tens column. Her answer will be 53.

$$7 + \cancel{5} + \cancel{9} + 8 + \cancel{4} + 5 + \cancel{9} + \cancel{6} = 53$$

Comments

When you read this through for the first time, the process may sound complicated. Therefore, first try the procedure out for yourself before explaining it to your child. This number trick can be used in the same way to add the digits in the tens and hundreds columns of two-digit and three-digit numbers so that you will not have to keep track of hundreds or thousands.

From *Helping Children with Mathematics, Grades 3–5*, published by GoodYearBooks. Copyright © 1996 James Riley, Marge Eberts, and Peggy Gisler.

From *Helping Children with Mathematics, Grades 3–5*, published by GoodYearBooks. Copyright © 1996 James Riley, Marge Eberts, and Peggy Gisler.

Materials

A clear mind
Loose beans, bean
   sticks, and bean
   flats (see Place
   Value Activity 1)

Addition Activity 5

It's All in Your Mind

(age 8 and older)

Procedure

This activity demonstrates two strategies for mental arithmetic. When people attempt mental arithmetic, they often try to follow the same procedures they would use with paper and pencil. This is very difficult to do. Mental arithmetic requires its own set of procedures.

1. Front-end addition

When adding with paper and pencil, children begin on the right by adding the ones. When adding with their minds, they should start on the left. For example, find the sum 35 + 22. First, add the 3 tens and 2 tens. Your child now knows that the sum must be fifty-something. Next, the 5 ones and 2 ones are added to equal 7. The sum is 57. Have your child try this with the following sums:

23 + 31	42 + 14	52 + 26
34 + 32	54 + 35	37 + 41

Note: When using front end addition, you should always check the ones digits to see if their sum exceeds 10. If the sum is greater than 10, then the sum of the digits in the tens place must be increased by one. For example, for the sum 57 + 36, the 5 tens of 57 and the 3 tens of 36 result in 8 tens. But 7 ones plus 6 ones adds to 1 ten and 3 ones. Thus there will be 9 tens and 3 ones.

2. Make a nice number

This method is used when one of the numbers to be added ends in an 8 or 9. Here, borrow one or two from one of the numbers being added to make the other number a multiple of ten. For example, find the sum 98 + 17. You can borrow a 2 from the 17 making it 15. Then add the 2 to the 98 making it 100. Add 15 + 100. Your sum is 115.

When first working on this strategy with your child, you should model the procedure using loose beans, bean sticks, and bean flats. Have your child represent 98 and 17 with beans. Take 2 beans away from the 17 beans (1 bean stick and 7 beans) to get 15 beans (1 bean stick and 5 beans). Give those 2 beans to the 98 beans (9 bean sticks and 8 beans) to get 100 beans (10 bean sticks). Have her add the new bean configuration of 15 + 100 to get 115 (11 bean sticks and 5 beans).

Subtraction of Whole Numbers

Subtraction is mathematically related to addition; it is the reverse or opposite of addition. Like addition, the activities in this section move from students' understanding the subtraction of multidigit numbers to handling this type of problem from their mathematics textbooks. Since subtraction is more difficult than addition for most children, your child will need to repeat most of these activities several times.

Subtraction Activity 1

Trading Down

(age 8 and older)

▼

Procedure

This game can be played by two to four players. Each player will need a place value mat.

Have each player begin with the same amount on her place value mat, such as 1 red stick, 4 green sticks, 7 blue sticks, and 2 yellow sticks. Each player takes turns rolling a die. The die indicates the number of yellow sticks to remove from the place value mat.

Whenever a player has no more yellow sticks on her mat, she can trade one blue stick for three yellow sticks. Likewise, one green stick can be exchanged for three blue sticks and one red stick for three green sticks. A player can only make trades when she has no more sticks for a given color section on her mat. For example, the first die roll is a 4. Since she has only 2 yellow sticks on her mat, she will need to trade one blue stick for three yellow sticks in order to remove 4 yellow sticks from her mat. The first player to trade away all of her sticks is declared the "winner."

Further Work

The game described above has the players trading 3-for-1. The game can be played by trading any amount from 2-for-1 to 10-for-1. Play the game with one of these alternative trade rates. If trades of 6-for-1 or more are made, use a pair of dice to keep the game from becoming too long. The roll of the first die should name the number of blue sticks and the second die the number of yellow sticks.

Materials

A set of trading sticks and place value mats made in Place Value Activity 3

A pair of dice

Subtraction Activity 2

Bean Stick Subtraction

(age 8 or older)

From *Helping Children with Mathematics, Grades 3–5*, published by GoodYearBooks. Copyright © 1996 James Riley, Marge Eberts, and Peggy Gisler.

Materials

Loose beans, bean
  sticks, and bean
  flats (see Place
  Value Activity 1)
Pencil and paper
Your child's
  mathematics
  textbook

Procedure

Find a page in your child's mathematics textbook that contains subtraction problems with three-digit numbers such as 643 − 257. Have her find the difference (answer to a subtraction problem) in each problem by using the following procedure.

Your child should represent 643 in loose beans, bean sticks, and bean flats. Then, she should write the digits 2, 5, and 7 below the bean stick configurations as shown here.

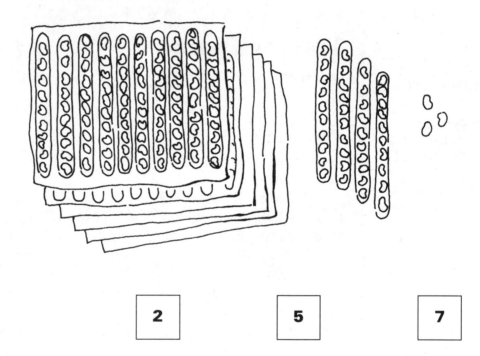

| 2 | 5 | 7 |

Then have her remove 257 beans from the 643 beans and place them next to the written digits. Notice that to do this your child will have to trade a bean flat for 10 bean sticks and a bean stick for 10 loose beans.

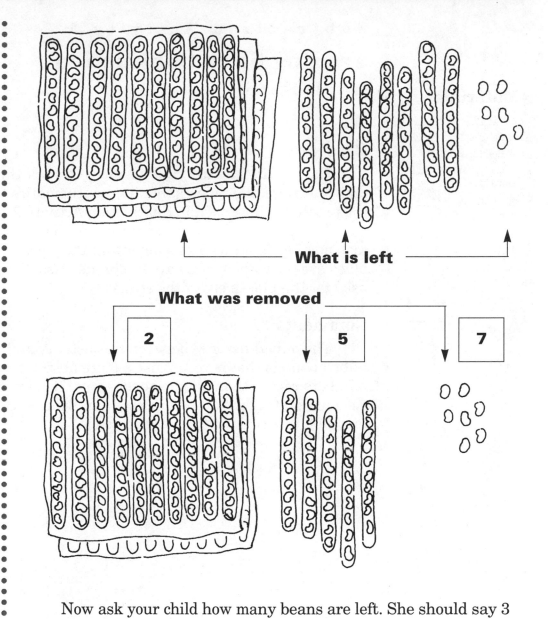

Now ask your child how many beans are left. She should say 3 bean flats, 8 bean sticks, and 6 loose beans to show a difference of 386.

Further Work

Also, the process can be reversed and the bean sticks can be joined again returning to the original position. Taking apart and putting together helps build the concept.

Comments

The placing of the bean sticks next to the written digits plays a very important role. It emphasizes the number that is being removed. Without this there is a tendency to toss the bean sticks back into the bean stick box where they become lost with all the other bean sticks. The use of the written digits and the placement of the sticks removed near these digits keeps the child's concentration on what has been removed and what is the difference.

Materials

A set of trading
  sticks and a place
  value mat made in
  Place Value
  Activity 3
Pencil and paper
Your child's
  mathematics
  textbook
_____
_____
_____

Trading Stick Subtraction

(age 8 and above)

▼

Procedure

Have your child use trading sticks to work through a set of three-digit subtraction problems from her mathematics textbook following the procedure described in Subtraction Activity 2.

In this activity, trading sticks are used to represent the numbers instead of bean sticks. Remember that the yellow sticks are ones, blues are tens, and greens are hundreds. Also, the place value mat is used for the placement of the sticks.

Comments

The only difference between this activity and Bean Stick Subtraction is that here you use a more abstract representation of numbers rather than a more obvious one. If your child has gained a good understanding of the process from Bean Stick Subtraction, you may find this activity to be unnecessary.

From *Helping Children with Mathematics, Grades 3–5*, published by GoodYearBooks. Copyright © 1996 James Riley, Marge Eberts, and Peggy Gisler.

From *Helping Children with Mathematics, Grades 3–5*, published by GoodYearBooks. Copyright © 1996 James Riley, Marge Eberts, and Peggy Gisler.

Chapter 2

Multiplication and Division of Whole Numbers

Multiplication is typically introduced toward the end of second grade but will be studied in greater depth in third, fourth, and fifth grades. Children do not usually encounter division until third grade and also continue working with this operation in fourth and fifth grades. In your children's mathematics classes, far more emphasis will be placed on understanding these two operations rather than doing laborious computations involving multiplying and dividing, which were so popular before the advent of the calculator.

Division is mathematically related to multiplication; it is the inverse or opposite of multiplication. If your child has a solid understanding of multiplication, he should be able to develop an understanding of the relationship between multiplication and division. Multiplication is used to check the answer to a quotient problem as well as to determine what the quotient is.

Basic Multiplication Facts

The learning of basic multiplication facts (1 x 1 through 9 x 9) can be very challenging. Many children seem unable to commit these facts to memory even after they have reached high school age. One reason for this may be because we spend too much time with rote drill and practice without first developing the underlying concepts for long-term retention.

The approach used in this book is different from traditional programs because it relies on building upon your child's understanding of previously learned facts. To accomplish this, the multiplication table has been divided into four regions.

X	1	2	3	4	5	6	7	8	9
1									
2									
3									
4				I					II
5									
6									
7									
8									
9				III					IV

The activities presented for each region of the table will help your child master the basic multiplication facts in ways that are natural and fun. In Region I, she will become familiar with the concept of multiplication through hands-on experiences. In the other regions, she will learn strategies for every possible multiplication combination. Finally, your child will be drilled for retention through a series of board games in which the whole family can participate.

From *Helping Children with Mathematics, Grades 3–5*, published by GoodYearBooks. Copyright © 1996 James Riley, Marge Eberts, and Peggy Gisler.

Basic Multiplication Activity 1
Making Multiplication Flash Cards
(age 8 and older)

From *Helping Children with Mathematics, Grades 3–5*, published by GoodYearBooks. Copyright © 1996 James Riley, Marge Eberts, and Peggy Gisler.

Materials

Set of index cards
Felt pen or crayons
Plastic adhesive
    paper (optional)

Procedure

Multiplication flash cards will be used in many of the activities in this chapter.

Write a basic multiplication fact on one side of an index card. Include all 81 basic facts, starting with 1 x 1 through 1 x 9 and continuing on to 9 x 9. **Do not include the answers (called products) anywhere on the cards, front or back.**

The backs of the index cards can be covered by plastic adhesive paper to make the cards look more attractive. They will also be more durable.

Comments

Commercial sets of cards always print the factors (numbers to be multiplied) on one side and the product on the other. This is not recommended. The answers should not be so readily available. The products should be determined by the learner and not given freely from outside sources such as answer sheets, teachers, parents, or calculators. Answers that come easily are not retained for a long period of time.

Region I

The easier multiplication facts are learned in this region through two models. They are called repeated addition and array models. The activities in this region develop the concept of multiplication through hands-on experiences.

Region I Activity 1

Repeated Addition

(age 8 and older)

▼

From *Helping Children with Mathematics, Grades 3–5*, published by GoodYearBooks. Copyright © 1996 James Riley, Marge Eberts, and Peggy Gisler.

Materials

Paper plates
Blocks, chips,
   buttons, or other
   counters
A set of multiplica-
   tion flash cards
   with the facts 1 x 1
   through 6 x 6
   made in Basic
   Multiplication
   Activity 1
Pencil and paper

Procedure

Have your child select a multiplication flash card at random, say 3 x 4. Have him lay out the number of paper plates equal to the first factor. Then, have him place the number of counters on each plate equal to the second factor.

Have your child count the total number of counters used. Ask, "How many counters did you use all together?" Have him write the fact 3 x 4 = 12.

Work through all of the flash cards following this procedure.

Further Work

Have your child randomly select a flash card, and write out the multiplication problem. If your child remembers the product, he should write it down. If he cannot recall the product, she should use the plates and counters to determine it. This procedure requires your child to be responsible for the correctness of his work and is more effective than you telling him the answer.

Comments

Multiplication problems are repeated addition problems. This means that 3 x 4 is the same as 4 + 4 + 4. To help your child see this concept, repeat the activity many times and relate real-life problems to the activity. For example, if each lunch box has 3 sandwiches and there are 4 lunch boxes, how many sandwiches could be eaten?

From *Helping Children with Mathematics, Grades 3–5*, published by GoodYearBooks. Copyright © 1996 James Riley, Marge Eberts, and Peggy Gisler.

Region I Activity 2

Arrays of Blocks

(age 8 and older)

▼

Procedure

Have your child select a multiplication fact from the stack of flash cards, like 3 x 4. Use a block array to illustrate the problem. For example:

Notice that the height of the block array is 3 and the length of the array is 4. Have your child count the number of blocks in the array above. The figure contains 12 blocks, so 3 x 4 = 12. Have him write out the fact and the product.

Construct block arrays for the entire set of multiplication facts.

Comments

The array model is the most important of the multiplication models. It is critical that your child learn the correct form for the model as it is needed for understanding concepts that will be developed later. The product in the array model is the number of blocks required to construct a rectangle whose dimensions are the factors. The fact 3 x 4 illustrated above shows the first factor, 3, in the vertical direction and the second factor, 4, in the horizontal direction.

Region I Activity 3

The Array Lattice

(age 8 and older)

From *Helping Children with Mathematics, Grades 3–5*, published by GoodYearBooks. Copyright © 1996 James Riley, Marge Eberts, and Peggy Gisler.

Materials

A set of multiplication flash cards with the facts 1 x 1 through 6 x 6 made in Basic Multiplication Activity 1

Pencil and paper

Procedure

Select a flash card at random, such as 2 x 6. Have your child draw 2 parallel horizontal lines. Then, have him draw 6 parallel vertical lines so that each intersects the 2 horizontal lines.

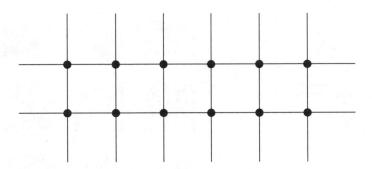

Have your child count the number of points of intersection. He should first count all the intersections in one line before moving on to another line. It makes no difference whether he chooses to count along the horizontal or vertical lines. Have him mark each intersection point with a dot as it is counted. The product is the number of points of intersection. In our example, there are 12 points.

Have your child write out the problem and the product. Continue with the other flash cards.

Further Work

Repeat the activity until your child has committed all the facts in Region I to memory. When doing this, have him write down the facts and products that he has learned. Use the array lattice model only if he cannot recall a fact.

Comments

The array lattice is just a quicker way to use the array model to determine basic multiplication facts.

Region I Activity 4

The Tic-Tac Game

(age 8 and older)

Materials

Tic-Tac game
  boards (see this
  book's insert)
A set of multiplica-
  tion flash cards
  with the facts 1 x 1
  through 6 x 6
  made in Basic
  Multiplication
  Activity 1
A set of markers
  such as bingo
  chips, dry lima
  beans, pennies,
  etc.

Procedure

This is a game that two to four players can play. Each player has a game board. To start, shuffle the flash cards and stack them upside down within easy reach of all players.

The first player draws a card from the top of the deck. The player tries to find the product of the factors on his game board. If there is a match, the player keeps the card and places a marker over the product on his board. If there is not a match, the player returns the card to the bottom of the card stack. It is then the next player's turn to draw. The winner is the player who completely covers his game board first.

To play again, exchange game boards so that each player will work with a different combination of multiplication facts.

41

Region II

When your child has mastered the facts in Region I, he is ready to tackle those in Region II. To help your child learn the Region II multiplication facts, a strategy based upon the distributive property will be taught.

The distributive property states that any multiplication fact can be expressed as the sum of two easier facts. For example, consider the multiplication fact 3 x 7. The factor 7 can be thought of as 3 + 4. Therefore, the distributive property says that:

$$3 \times 7 = 3 \times (3 + 4) = (3 \times 3) + (3 \times 4) = 9 + 12 = 21$$

While the distributive property can be used to determine multiplication products in any region, it is developed here because the property can easily build upon what your child has already learned in Region I. This strategy permits your child to represent a Region II multiplication fact as the sum of two Region I multiplication facts. The following activities teach the Region II multiplication facts using the distributive property.

Region II Activity 1

Distributive Property Modeled

(age 8 and older)

Materials

Blocks, tiles, or block cards (see page 126)

A set of multiplication flash cards with the facts 2 x 7, 2 x 8, 2 x 9, 3 x 7, 3 x 8, 3 x 9, 4 x 7, 4 x 8, 4 x 9, 5 x 7, 5 x 8, 5 x 9, 6 x 7, 6 x 8, and 6 x 9 made in Basic Multiplication Activity 1

Pencil and paper

Procedure

Select a flash card at random, like 3 x 7. Have your child construct a block array to illustrate the problem. Refer to Region I Activity 3 if you need instruction on how to make a block array model. The 3 x 7 array would look like this:

From *Helping Children with Mathematics, Grades 3–5*, published by GoodYearBooks. Copyright © 1996 James Riley, Marge Eberts, and Peggy Gisler.

Next, have your child break the array into two arrays. Make sure that he breaks the array at a point as close to the middle as possible.

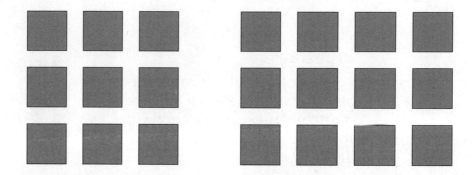

Ask your child to identify the multiplication fact shown by each of the small arrays and its product. The 3 x 3 array has 9 blocks and the 3 x 4 array has 12 blocks. Have him add the products of the two small arrays. This sum is equal to the product of the large array. Your child should write out his answers to help him keep track of what he is doing. The product of 3 x 7 is the sum of the 3 x 3 and 3 x 4 arrays.

$$3 \times 7 = 3 \times (3 + 4) = (3 \times 3) + (3 \times 4) = 9 + 12 = 21$$

Have your child reassemble the large array. Have him count all the blocks in the large array to confirm that the sum of the products of the two small arrays is equal to the product of the large array.

Repeat this procedure for the set of multiplication flash cards.

From *Helping Children with Mathematics, Grades 3–5*, published by GoodYearBooks. Copyright © 1996 James Riley, Marge Eberts, and Peggy Gisler.

From *Helping Children with Mathematics, Grades 3–5*, published by GoodYearBooks. Copyright © 1996 James Riley, Marge Eberts, and Peggy Gisler.

Region II Activity 2

Distributive Property Pictured

(age 8 and older)

▼

Materials

Procedure

Select a multiplication flash card at random, say 4 x 8. Have your child make a block array to show the multiplication fact on the card.

Next, have him draw a rectangle with height and length of the figure labeled to correspond to the dimensions of the block array. The labeled rectangle for 4 x 8 should look like this:

Have your child divide the block array into two arrays as in Region II Activity 1. Then, he should draw a line through the rectangle dividing it just like he divided the block array. Have him label the dimensions of the two small rectangles.

Inside each small rectangle, he should write the multiplication fact and product it represents. In this case, 4 x 4 = 16 should be written in both rectangles. These products are called partial products. Now, the rectangle should look like this:

Have your child find the sum of the partial products. Have him write down the discovered fact 4 x 8 = 32.

Work through the multiplication flash cards finding the products as above.

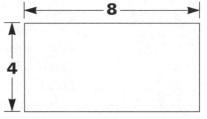

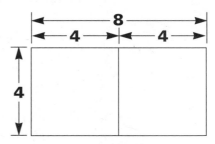

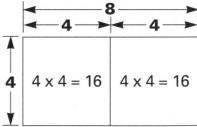

Comments

This activity builds upon the previous one by extending your child's knowledge of the distributive property from concrete towards abstraction. This activity may be skipped, if your child gained a solid understanding of the process in Distributive Property Modeled.

Region II Activity 3

The Distributive Property as Procedure

(age 8 and older)

Procedure

Have your child select a flash card at random. If he knows the fact, he should write out the problem and product. Many parents and teachers have a child only recite a fact. The child should also write the problem and the correct product. This reinforces the learning by having the child say, see, and write the fact.

If your child does not know the fact, have him follow this procedure. Assume he draws the card 3 x 7. The second factor, in this case 7, can be broken up into two numbers such as 3 and 4. Following the distributive property, the multiplication fact, 3 x 7, can be broken up into two simpler multiplication facts, 3 x 3 and 3 x 4. Have your child illustrate this as shown below.

$$3 \times 7 \begin{cases} 3 = 3 \times 3 \\ 4 = 3 \times 4 \end{cases}$$

Have him find the products of 3 x 3 and 3 x 4. Then, have him find the sum of the two products. The answer is 21.

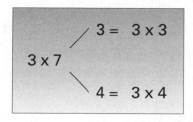

Have your child continue with this activity until all of the multiplication facts in Region II have been learned.

Comments

This activity provides your child with a fast way to determine unlearned multiplication facts found in Region II. The distributive property is used in an abstract manner as your child is not representing the facts with models.

Materials

A set of multiplication flash cards with the facts 2 x 7, 2 x 8, 2 x 9, 3 x 7, 3 x 8, 3 x 9, 4 x 7, 4 x 8, 4 x 9, 5 x 7, 5 x 8, 5 x 9, 6 x 7, 6 x 8, and 6 x 9 made in Basic Multiplication Activity 1

Pencil and paper

Region III

Your child has now learned all of the basic multiplication facts found in Regions I and II. The multiplication facts in Region III are very easy to learn since they are exactly the same as those in Region II except that the order of the factors is reversed. For example, 3 x 7 is a Region II fact and 7 x 3 is a Region III fact. All your child needs to learn is that a x b is the same as b x a, the commutative property of multiplication.

The commutative property of multiplication applies to all multiplication facts. It is developed here because your child can discover that by having learned the Region II facts he also learned the Region III facts. When your child understands that 3 x 7 = 7 x 3, he reduces by nearly one-half the number of facts he must commit to memory. The following activity will help your child make this connection.

Region III Activity 1

The Commutative Property

(age 8 and older)

Materials

Blocks, tiles, or block cards (see page 126)

A set of multiplication flash cards with the facts 7 x 2, 7 x 3, 7 x 4, 7 x 5, 7 x 6, 8 x 2, 8 x 3, 8 x 4, 8 x 5, 8 x 6, 9 x 2, 9 x 3, 9 x 4, 9 x 5, and 9 x 6 made in Basic Multiplication Activity 1

Pencil and paper

Procedure

Select a flash card at random, like 7 x 3. Have your child construct a block array to illustrate the problem. Refer to Region I Activity 3 if you need instruction on how to make a block array model. The 7 x 3 array would look like this:

Have your child write out the fact and the product. In this case, he should write 7 x 3 = 21.

Next, have him reconstruct the block array to illustrate 3 x 7. The 3 x 7 array would look like this:

Have your child write out the fact and the product. He should write 3 x 7 = 21. Have him observe that reversing the factors results in the same product. Finally, have him write out both the original problem and the commutated, or re-ordered, problem. For example:

> 7 x 3 = 3 x 7 = 21

Work through the set of multiplication flash cards.

From *Helping Children with Mathematics, Grades 3–5*, published by GoodYearBooks. Copyright © 1996 James Riley, Marge Eberts, and Peggy Gisler.

Region IV

Your child is now ready to proceed to the facts in Region IV. Unfortunately, there is no simple single strategy that works for all the facts in this region. However, two strategies, magic nines and the associative property, seem to work fairly well and cover all facts except 7 x 7. You can have your child learn the 7 x 7 fact using Region I Activity 3. There is an activity for each strategy in Region IV.

Region IV Activity 1

The Magic Nines

(age 8 and older)

Procedure

The Magic Nines strategy works in this way:

1. Write the problem with the 9 as the second factor. For example, write 9 x 7 as 7 x 9.

2. The first digit of a nines product is one less than the multiplier (the number that multiplies another number). For example, with 8 x 9 = 72, the 7 of 72 is one smaller than the multiplier 8.

3. The sum of the digits in a nines product always adds up to 9. With the product 72, the two digits add up to 9, 7 + 2 = 9.

Have your child pick a nines fact flash card at random, like 6 x 9. To find the first digit of the product, ask him, "What number is one smaller than the multiplier 6?" Have him write the answer, 5, in the first digit position. To find the second digit ask your child, "What number added to 5 equals 9?" Have him write his response, 4, to the right of the first digit to show the product of 6 x 9 is 54. Have your child work his way through the nines facts using the Magic Nines strategy.

Comments

Although your child learned some of the nines multiplication facts in earlier regions, have him look at them again using this strategy so he can decide which strategies work best for him.

Any number whose digit sum is a multiple of nine is itself a multiple of nine. If nine divides the sum of the digits of a number, it will divide the number. Is 396 a multiple of nine? The sum of the digits is 3 + 9 + 6 = 18. Nine divides into 18, so it will divide into 396. Thus, 396 is a multiple of 9. (Use a calculator and check this out.)

Materials

A set of multiplication flash cards with the facts 1 x 9, 2 x 9, 3 x 9, 4 x 9, 5 x 9, 6 x 9, 7 x 9, 8 x 9, 9 x 7, 9 x 8, and 9 x 9 made in Basic Multiplication Activity 1

Pencil and paper

From *Helping Children with Mathematics, Grades 3–5*, published by GoodYearBooks. Copyright © 1996 James Riley, Marge Eberts, and Peggy Gisler.

The Associative Property

(age 8 or older)

Materials

A set of multiplication flash cards with the facts 7 x 8, 7 x 9, 8 x 7, and 8 x 8 made in Basic Multiplication Activity 1

Pencil and paper

Procedure

The associative property states that **a x (b x c) = (a x b) x c.** This property provides a strategy for your child to solve facts like 7 x 8 and 8 x 9. While the associative property can determine products in any region, it is developed here because the property uses facts learned in previous regions. This activity will help your child learn this relation.

Have your child select a multiplication flash card, say 8 x 7. Point out to him that 8 = 2 x 4. Therefore, 8 x 7 = 2 x 4 x 7. Remind your child that 4 x 7 is a fact he learned in Region II. Have him tell you the product of 4 x 7, 28. Show him that 2 x 4 x 7 is equal to 2 x 28. And 2 x 28 is two 28s or 28 + 28 = 56. Thus, 8 x 7 = 56.

These steps can be summarized in the following written procedure.

$$
8 \times 7 = 2 \times 4 \times 7 = 2 \times 28 = \quad
\begin{array}{r}
28 \\
+\ 28 \\
\hline
56
\end{array}
$$

Have him work through the set of multiplication flash cards using the above written procedure for the associative property.

From *Helping Children with Mathematics, Grades 3–5*, published by GoodYearBooks. Copyright © 1996 James Riley, Marge Eberts, and Peggy Gisler.

All Regions

Your child now knows strategies for determining the basic multiplication facts. He will still need considerable drill work to commit them firmly to his memory. The following activities are games that drill children on the multiplication facts. Play them with your children as the games are fun for the whole family.

All Regions Activity 1

The Advanced Tic-Tac Game

(age 8 and older)

▼

Materials

Advanced Tic-Tac game boards (see this book's insert)
A complete set of multiplication flash cards made in Basic Multiplication Activity 1
A set of markers like bingo chips, dry lima beans, pennies, etc.

Procedure

Two to four players can play this game. Each player has a game board. Shuffle the flash cards and place them stacked upside down within easy reach of all players.

The first player draws a card from the top of the deck. The player tries to find the product of the factors on his game board. If there is a match, the player keeps the card and places a marker over the product on his game board. If there is not a match, the player returns the card to the bottom of the card stack. Then, it is the next player's turn. The winner is the player who completely covers his game board first.

To play again, exchange game boards so that each player will work with a different combination of multiplication facts.

All Regions Activity 2
Play Multiplication Scramble
(age 8 and older)

Materials

A copy of the
multiplication
Scramble table
(as shown in
the insert)
A complete set of
multiplication
flash cards made
in Basic
Multiplication
Activity 1
Pencil and paper

Procedure

Shuffle the flash cards and deal seven cards to each player. Place the remaining cards upside down to form a drawing pile. A flash card is drawn from the stack and its product is written on the blank Multiplication Scramble table. This product is the starting point of the game.

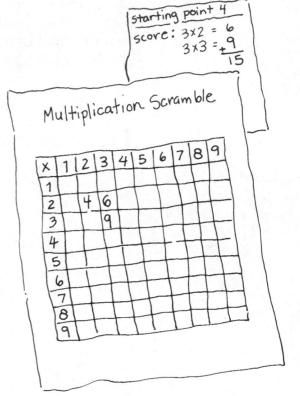

The first player begins by playing any of his flash cards that has a product that shares an edge with the starting point. The player puts played flash cards in his own stack.

For example, when 2 x 2 is turned over, 4 is the starting point as shown below. A player, holding the 3 x 2 flash card would write 6 in the multiplication table as it is next to 4. Also, if that player holds the 3 x 3 flash card it can be played since its product 9 is next to the 6.

Each player continues until he is no longer able to play a flash card which has a fact that shares an edge with the starting point or a previously played product. When a player has made all possible product placements in a turn, the score is computed as the sum of the flash cards played. In our example, the player's score would be: 3 x 2 + 3 x 3 or 15.

At the end of the turn, the player draws enough flash cards from the drawing pile to replace the ones he played. Players continue to draw from the pile until no more flash cards remain.

If a player cannot place a product on the table, the turn is lost and play continues with the next player.

The game is over when the Multiplication Scramble table is filled. Tally up each player's total score for all turns. The winner of the game is the player with the highest sum of placed products.

From *Helping Children with Mathematics, Grades 3–5*, published by GoodYearBooks. Copyright © 1996 James Riley, Marge Eberts, and Peggy Gisler.

All Regions Activity 3
Play Multipaths

(age 8 and older)

▼

From *Helping Children with Mathematics, Grades 3–5*, published by GoodYearBooks. Copyright © 1996 James Riley, Marge Eberts, and Peggy Gisler.

Materials

A Multipaths play-
ing board (see this
book's insert)
Three sets of dry
lima beans, one
set
colored red,
another blue, and
the third green
A set of multiplica-
tion flash cards
with the facts
2 x 2 to 2 x 9,
3 x 3 to 3 x 9,
4 x 4 to 4 x 9,

5 x 5 to 5 x 9,
6 x 6 to 6 x 9,
7 x 7, 7 x 8, 7 x 9,
8 x 8, 8 x 9, and
9 x 9 made in
Basic Multiplica-
tion Activity 1
Four cards the
same size as the
flash cards and
marked with the
word "switch"

Procedure

The object of the game is to build a path of colored beans across the game board. The free hexagon in the center of the playing board is considered a part of every player's path.

Each player selects a color and gathers all beans of that color as playing pieces. Shuffle the multiplication flash cards and the "switch" cards together and deal each player three cards. Stack the remaining cards upside down to form a drawing pile.

The first player draws a card from the top of the pile and puts it in his hand. The player then selects one of his four cards and recites the basic multiplication fact shown on that card and the product. The player lays one of his colored beans on the game board on a hexagon that shows the recited product. Place the card on the discard pile. The next player completes a turn in the same way.

If a player plays a "switch" card, he can remove any one of another player's colored beans from the game board and replace it with one of his own.

The winner is the first player who builds a path of hexagons containing his colored beans joining the sides of the board displaying his color.

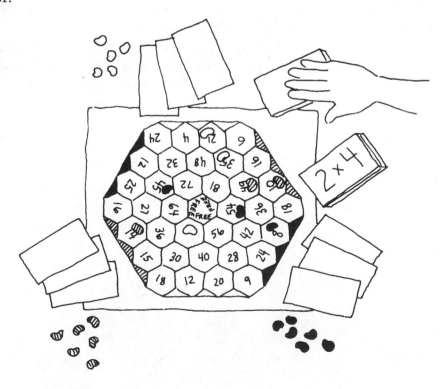

All Regions Activity 4

Factor Codes

(age 8 and older)

Procedure

Designate one player to be the coder. The coder shuffles the ten number cards and places each one with the question mark side up below one of the lettered positions on the cardboard strip.

A	B	C	D	E	F	G	H	I	J
?	?	?	?	?	?	?	?	?	?

Each player, in turn, asks the product of the cards for any two lettered positions. The coder looks at the cards without letting the other players see them. Then, the coder tells the player(s) what the product is for those two lettered positions. The coder does not tell what the factors of the product are. Whenever a player thinks he knows a factor, he can announce it to the coder. The coder will tell him whether he is right or wrong. Play continues until all the factors for the lettered positions have been found.

The player who correctly identified the most lettered positions is the winner.

Further Work

Here is an alternate version of the game to try. In this game, the winner is the first person to correctly identify all the numbers for each lettered position. Play is the same as above except players do not announce factors as they find them, only when they believe they have discovered the factors for all of the lettered positions.

Materials

A set of ten cards, each with one of the ten digits, 0–9, printed on one side and a question mark lettered on the other side

A cardboard strip with ten lettered positions as shown below

Pencil and paper

The Multiplication Algorithm

Your children only need to learn how to handle multiplication problems with one or two digit multipliers, like 3 x 35 and 57 x 27 with pencil and paper computation. Problems with three or more digits should be done with a calculator. The activities in this section will concentrate on the development of the multiplication algorithm (step-by-step procedures for solving a problem) with one or two digits. The emphasis will be on concept development rather than just rote exercise.

Multiplication Activity 1

Bean Stick Multiplication

(age 9 and older)

Materials

Loose beans, bean sticks, and bean flats (see Place Value Activity 1) Pencil and paper

Procedure

Have your child represent the multiplication problem 3 x 17 using loose beans and bean sticks as shown below.

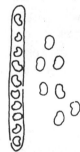 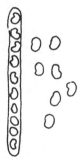

Next, have your child combine all the loose beans and count them. If the sum of loose beans is ten or more, then ten beans should be traded for a bean stick. In this case, 20 loose beans can be exchanged for 2 bean sticks. Now he should combine all the bean sticks and count them. If the sum of the beans sticks is ten or more, then 10 bean sticks should be traded for a bean flat. With this example, 5 bean sticks cannot be traded for a flat. Finally, count the flats.

After all trading is completed, there should be 5 bean sticks and one loose bean for 51. This means that 3 x 17 = 51.

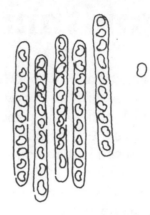

Have your child work the following problems using this procedure.

3 x 14	2 x 17	2 x 18	3 x 19	3 x 24	3 x 25
2 x 26	3 x 27	2 x 28	3 x 29	4 x 34	3 x 35
2 x 36	3 x 37	2 x 38	2 x 39	4 x 43	3 x 46

Further Work

The next step for your child is to relate the bean stick representation to a pencil and paper computation. Many mathematics programs use the following procedure as a transitional pencil and paper algorithm.

Have your child work through the problems again using the pencil and paper procedure.

Bean Sticks	Loose Beans	
1	7	
x	3	
2	1	= 3 x 7 Loose Beans
3		= 3 x 1 Bean Stick
5	1	

Comments

The repeated addition model introduced in Region I Activity 1 is used to develop the ideas in this activity. That is, the problem 3 x 17 means 17 + 17 + 17.

From *Helping Children with Mathematics, Grades 3–5*, published by GoodYearBooks. Copyright © 1996 James Riley, Marge Eberts, and Peggy Gisler.

Multiplication Activity 2

Base Blocks

(age 9 and older)

▼

Procedure

Base blocks can be used with the array model of multiplication to help children learn the concept of two-digit multiplication. Find a page in your child's mathematics textbook that contains multiplication problems with two digits, like 23 × 24. Have him find the products of each problem using the following procedure.

Your child should make a 23 × 24 array using base blocks as shown below.

Collect the base blocks together, flats, longs, and units. Have your child make appropriate trades as a flat for 10 longs and a long for 10 units. When all possible trades have been made, have your child write the number represented by the base blocks. In this case, he should write 552 which represents the 5 flats, 5 longs, and 2 units.

Further Work

The base block array model of a two-digit by two-digit multiplication problem can be related to pencil and paper computation. This

Materials

A set of base
  blocks (see page
  20)
Pencil and paper
Your child's
  mathematics
  textbook

relation will make the pencil and paper procedure less rule oriented and more concrete.

Rework the problems using the pencil and paper procedure.

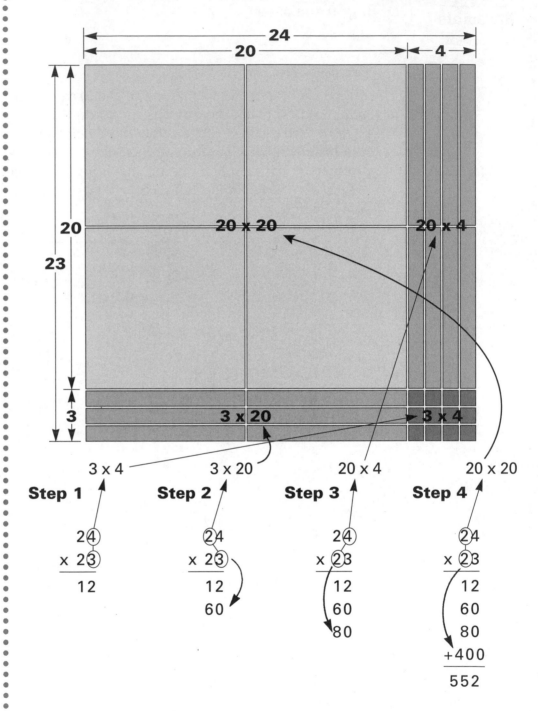

From *Helping Children with Mathematics, Grades 3–5*, published by GoodYearBooks. Copyright © 1996 James Riley, Marge Eberts, and Peggy Gisler.

The Meaning of Division

Do you remember working through long division problems like 38,529 divided by 839? With the access of inexpensive calculators, there is no need for your children to possess the skills to solve such division problems. However, it is very important for children to develop the concept of division and to understand the division algorithm.

The first activities will develop an understanding of the division concept using two models. They are called measurement and partition models. The two models illustrate how a division problem can describe two different situations. The measurement model shows the number of sets that can be made from an amount. The partition model shows the number of items within each set of an amount that is shared equally. Repeat these activities a number of times until your child is comfortable with the division models. Later activities will develop a procedure to perform long division easily first using the partition model and then pencil and paper computation. Several games are used in this section to make practicing division fun.

Division Activity 1

Give Everyone the Same

(age 8 and above)

Procedure

Have your child count out 36 beans. Of these 36, have him count out 4 beans and place them in a tub. Have him count out 4 more beans and place them in another tub. Continue this process until all 36 beans have been placed in a tub. Ask your child, "How many tubs contain beans?" In this case, 9 tubs contain beans.

Have your child place beans in tubs to complete the chart using the same procedure.

# of beans	12	16	18	18	24	24	36	48
# of beans per tub	3	4	2	3	3	4	6	6
# of tubs with beans	?	?	?	?	?	?	?	?

Show your child the mathematical relation between division and multiplication. Point out that the divisor (the number that divides

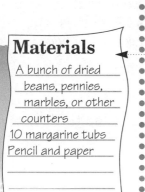

Materials

A bunch of dried
    beans, pennies,
    marbles, or other
    counters
10 margarine tubs
Pencil and paper

another number), 4, and the quotient (the answer to a division problem), 9, are the factors in the multiplication problem.

> # of beans ÷ # of beans per tub = # of tubs with beans
>
> 36 ÷ 4 = 9
>
> # of tubs with beans x # of beans per tub = # of beans
>
> 9 x 4 = 36

Now, have your child fill out the above chart again using his understanding of the mathematical relation. Have him first write out the multiplication problem and then solve it. In our example, he should write out □ x 4 = 36, and then put the answer 9 in the □. Finally, have him write out the corresponding division relation, 36 ÷ 4 = 9.

Repeat this activity using different numbers of beans and beans per tub. Be sure to select numbers that do not leave any remainders.

Further Work

Try the procedure using numbers in the chart that will leave remainders. For example, with 29 beans and 5 beans per tub, there will be 5 tubs with beans and 4 beans left over.

Create story problems that relate the procedure to real life situations for your child to solve. For example: John has 12 cookies. He places them into packages of 3 each. How many packages of cookies will he have? John will have 4 packages of cookies.

Comments

This activity uses the measurement model to develop the concept of division. The measurement model answers the question, "How many sets are there?"

From *Helping Children with Mathematics, Grades 3–5*, published by GoodYearBooks. Copyright © 1996 James Riley, Marge Eberts, and Peggy Gisler.

Division Activity 2

Everyone Shares Fairly

(age 8 and above)

From *Helping Children with Mathematics, Grades 3–5*, published by GoodYearBooks. Copyright © 1996 James Riley, Marge Eberts, and Peggy Gisler.

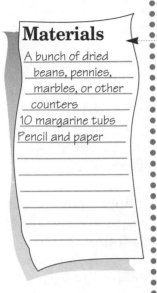

Materials

A bunch of dried
  beans, pennies,
  marbles, or other
  counters
10 margarine tubs
Pencil and paper

Procedure

Ask your child to count out 36 beans. Have him divide the 36 beans equally among 9 tubs. After he has distributed the beans, ask, "How many counters are in each tub?" In this case, the answer is 4 beans.

Have him fill out the following chart using the same procedure.

# of beans	12	16	18	18	24	24	36	48
# of tubs with beans	4	4	9	6	8	6	6	6
# of beans per tub	?	?	?	?	?	?	?	?

Ask your child to rework the chart using the mathematical relation between division and multiplication as in Division Activity 1. For our example, he should write out $\square \times 9 = 36$, place the answer 4 in the $\square$, and then write $36 \div 9 = 4$.

Ask your child to explain the difference between what he did in this activity and Division Activity 1. Refer back to the explanation in the Meaning of Division, if necessary.

Repeat the activity using different numbers of beans and tubs. Be sure to select numbers that do not leave any remainders.

Further Work

Try the procedure using numbers of beans and tubs that will leave remainders. For example, with 26 beans and 3 tubs, there will be 8 beans in each tub and 2 beans left over.

Relate this procedure to real-life situations. Make up story problems for your child to work. For example: Jeff has a giant 20-slice pizza. He wants to share the slices equally with his three friends. How many slices would Jeff and each friend get? Jeff and his friends would each get five slices.

Comments

This activity uses the partition model to develop the concept of division. The partition model answers the question "If a number of things are to be shared equally among a number of sharers, how many things would each sharer get?" The partition model is also known as the fair sharing model.

Division Activity 3

Play Divingo

(age 8 and older)

Procedure

This game is tic-tac-toe with a twist—you have to solve a division problem to claim a square.

Each player needs a Divingo game sheet. Shuffle the cards and place them in a drawing pile with the numeral side face down.

Draw a card from the pile, and lay it face up next to the pile. Each player writes that numeral anywhere on his Divingo game sheet. Once the numeral has been placed, the player cannot move it to another position. Players take turns drawing cards from the pile. The first player to complete three division problems in a row, a column, or a diagonal is the winner. If the cards are all played before anyone wins, shuffle and go through the cards again. A winning Divingo game sheet could look like this.

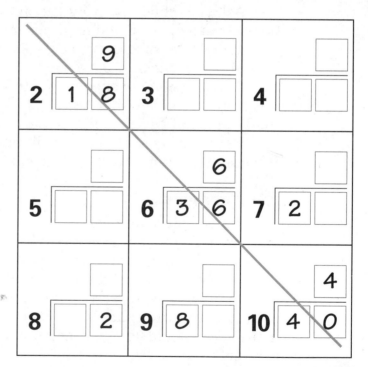

To play again, use a new Divingo game sheet or create your own game sheet by changing the position of the divisors.

Comments

Divingo provides excellent practice in solving simple division problems.

From *Helping Children with Mathematics, Grades 3–5*, published by GoodYearBooks. Copyright © 1996 James Riley, Marge Eberts, and Peggy Gisler.

Division Activity 4

Play Cross Out

(age 8 and older)

From *Helping Children with Mathematics, Grades 3–5*, published by GoodYearBooks. Copyright © 1996 James Riley, Marge Eberts, and Peggy Gisler.

Materials

A set of Cross Out
game sheets
(see page 128)
A set of 36 cards
numbered 1
through 9—each
number will appear
on four cards
Pencil

Procedure

Each player needs a different Cross Out game sheet. Shuffle the cards and place them with the numeral side facedown in a drawing pile.

A player picks up the top card and reads the number on it out loud. If the called number divides evenly a number on the player's game sheet, then the player may select a number to cross out on his game sheet. To cross out the selected number, the player must recite the correct division problem and answer, otherwise he loses the turn. Each player can only cross out one number on his game sheet for a called card, even though that card's number might divide evenly into another number on his sheet.

The first player to cross out all the numbers on his game sheet is the winner.

To play again, swap game sheets or create your own.

Comments

Beside providing practice with division, Cross Out is an exercise in finding factors of composite numbers. A composite number is a number other than zero or one that has more than two different factors. For example, 10 is a composite number because it has four factors 1, 2, 5, and 10, while 11 is not because it only has two factors 1 and 11.

Division Activity 5

Trading in for Long Division

(age 9 and older)

Materials

Loose beans, bean
sticks, and bean
flats (see Place
Value Activity 1)
Pencil and paper
Your child's
mathematics
textbook

Procedure

Find a page in your child's mathematics textbook that has division problems with one digit divisors like 744 ÷ 6. Ask your child to represent the dividend using the loose beans, bean sticks, and bean flats. The dividend 744 would be represented as follows.

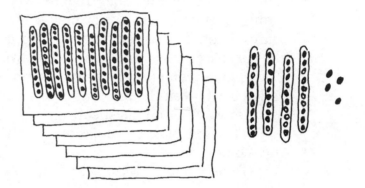

Lay out six sheets of paper. Have your child divide the bean flats, bean sticks, and loose beans representing 744 by placing equal amounts on each of the six sheets of paper. To do this, have him follow this procedure:

Step 1: Divide the bean flats equally between the sheets of paper.

Remaining:

Step 2: Trade any remaining bean flats into bean sticks.

From *Helping Children with Mathematics, Grades 3–5*, published by GoodYearBooks. Copyright © 1996 James Riley, Marge Eberts, and Peggy Gisler.

Step 3: Divide the bean sticks equally between the sheets of paper.

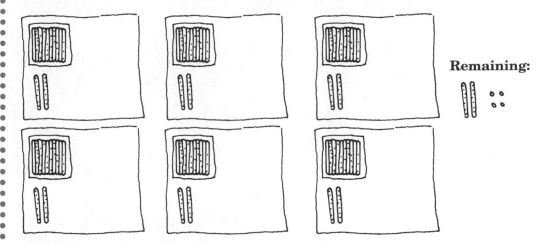

Remaining:

Step 4: Trade any remaining bean sticks for loose beans.

Step 5: Divide the loose beans equally between the sheets of paper.

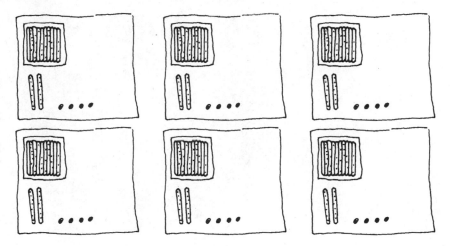

Your child needs to learn how to relate the above concept to pencil and paper computation.

Step 1: 1 bean flat on each of the six sheets of paper for a total of 6 bean flats.

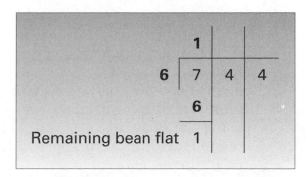

Step 3: 2 bean sticks on each of the six sheets of paper for a total of 12 bean sticks.

```
              1   2
         6 |  7   4   4
              6
              1   4
              1   2
 Remaining bean sticks    2
```

Step 5: 4 beans on each of the six sheets of paper for a total of 24 loose beans.

```
              1   2   4
         6 |  7   4   4
              6
              1   4
              1   2
                  2   4
                  2   4
 Remaining loose beans        0
```

Have your child do several problems relating the bean stick representation to pencil and paper computation.

Comments

This activity builds on the ideas explored in Division Activity 2: Everyone Shares Fairly. In that activity, an amount of beans was divided equally among a specified number of tubs. Here, an amount represented by bean sticks was divided equally among sheets of paper using the same concept. Also, your child will learn in this activity to relate long division concepts with pencil and paper computation procedures.

From *Helping Children with Mathematics, Grades 3–5*, published by GoodYearBooks. Copyright © 1996 James Riley, Marge Eberts, and Peggy Gisler.

Division Activity 6

Play High Quotient

(age 10 and older)

Materials

A set of 30 cards
numbered
0 to 9 — each
number will appear
on three cards
Pencil and paper

Procedure

Each player draws a "blank" division problem as shown below on a sheet of paper.

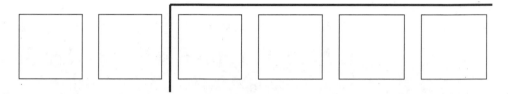

Shuffle the numbered cards and place them upside down in a drawing pile.

To begin play, the first player turns over the top card from the drawing pile. The player writes the card's numeral someplace in a square on his blank division problem. Players take turns drawing a card and writing it on their blank division problem. Play stops when each player has filled in all the squares of his blank division problem.

Each player then finds the quotient for his division problem. After completing the division computation, a calculator may be used to check the correctness of the division. Point out to your child that when he uses the calculator to divide, the remainder, if any, is shown as a decimal. The player whose division problem has the highest quotient is the winner.

All Operations

The next two activities combine the operations of addition, subtraction, multiplication, and division. These activities help develop "number sense." All of the operations must be used in cooperation with each other to solve the number puzzles. As your children learn more mathematics, they can revise the games to include the new concepts.

All Operations Activity 1

Mrs. Gaylord's Fifth-Grade Game*

(age 10 and older)

Materials

Calendar

Pencil and paper

Procedure

Mrs. Gaylord's fifth-grade class meets the following challenge every day. Each day she writes the date on the chalkboard using its numeral representation. For example, March 12, 1994, is 3/12/94.

Her class uses the digits 3–1–2–9–4 to make an equation (a mathematical sentence using the = sign). The digits must be kept in order but can be combined to make other numbers, like using the 1 and 2 to get 12. Any operation can be used. Mrs. Gaylord's class tries to find as many combinations as possible. Here are some combinations for 3–1–2–9–4.

$$3 \times 12 = 9 \times 4 \qquad (3 \times 1) + 2 = 9 - 4 \qquad (3 \times 12) \div 9 = 4$$

You can play Mrs. Gaylord's game with all kinds of dates. Try this game using famous dates, like December 7, 1941, or family birthdates. Note that for some dates an equation cannot be made.

* Used with permission from Judy Gaylord, Kalamazoo, Michigan.

From *Helping Children with Mathematics, Grades 3–5*, published by GoodYearBooks. Copyright © 1996 James Riley, Marge Eberts, and Peggy Gisler.

All Operations Activity 2

Challenge Solitaire

(age 10 and older)

Materials

A deck of playing cards

Pencil and paper

Procedure

The object of the game is to combine the number values of the playing cards in any order using any operation to make the value of 100.

The playing cards have been given these number values:

> Aces = 1
>
> 2–10 = Number value shown on the card
>
> Jacks = 11
>
> Queens = 12
>
> Kings = 13

Shuffle the deck of playing cards. Start play by dealing yourself cards one at a time. Keep dealing cards until you can make the value of 100 out of the cards you have dealt. Try to make 100 using the fewest cards possible.

To make 100 with the cards dealt, follow these rules:

> 1. Every card dealt must be used.
> 2. The cards can be used in any order.
> 3. Any operation can be used.

For example, if the cards dealt are:

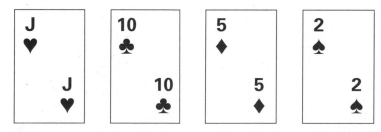

Those cards can be arranged as follows to make 100.

> (Jack x 10) – (5 x 2) = (11 x 10) – 10 = 110 – 10 = 100

Work through the entire deck of playing cards. If needed, turn the last card in the deck into a wild card (any number) to make the final 100.

Further Work

As your child becomes more experienced with mathematics, have him try this solitaire game, which was created by Art White, a teacher, mathematician, and composer of music.*

The object of the game is to combine the number values on five cards in any way using any operation to equal 100.

The cards use the same numerical values as in Challenge Solitaire. Shuffle a deck of playing cards and discard the top two cards. Deal yourself five cards. For example, if the cards dealt are 10, 4, 3, 2, and 8, they could be arranged like this to equal 100.

$$10^2 \times (3 - 8/4) = 100 \times (3 - 2) = 100 \times 1 = 100$$

After a solution has been found for the first five cards, take the next five cards from the top of the deck and repeat the challenge. The game is won if the player can work through the whole deck, meeting each challenge.

* Used by permission of Professor Arthur White, Kalamazoo, Michigan.

From *Helping Children with Mathematics, Grades 3–5*, published by GoodYearBooks. Copyright © 1996 James Riley, Marge Eberts, and Peggy Gisler.

From *Helping Children with Mathematics, Grades 3–5*, published by GoodYearBooks. Copyright © 1996 James Riley, Marge Eberts, and Peggy Gisler.

## Chapter 3

Fractions, Decimals, and Percents

We do not use fractions as much as we did at one time. Today's world is a computer world, and computers do their arithmetic with decimals rather than fractions. Another reason for less emphasis on fractions is the increased acceptance of the metric system of measurement, which is a decimal system, not a fractional system.

The fraction 3/4 represents the same number as the decimal 0.75. Only the system of symbols is different. Children need to learn how to use both systems. Then when they clearly understand the concepts of fractions and decimals, they are ready to learn about the related concept of percent which expresses the same relationship in hundredths. While the emphasis in this chapter is on fractions, the use of decimals and percents in daily life will also be explored.

The Fraction Concept

An understanding of fractions is still very important. Fractions are used in important activities such as cooking, sewing, and carpentry. Knowing how to handle fractions helps children learn algebra because the rules for algebraic manipulation are exactly the same as those for fractions. Another reason for studying fractions is that they provide a perfect model for the study of probability.

The study of fractions should be limited to the development of concepts and manipulations of simple fractions that children may encounter in day-to-day living. The activities in this section concentrate on concept development and are limited to simple, easy-to-understand fractions.

Fraction Concept Activity 1

Making Fraction Pieces

(age 8 or older)

From *Helping Children with Mathematics, Grades 3–5*, published by GoodYearBooks. Copyright © 1996 James Riley, Marge Eberts, and Peggy Gisler.

Materials

Fraction pieces
 (see page 129)
Cardboard
Scissors
Glue

Procedure

Fraction pieces will be used in almost all of the fraction activities in this chapter.

Make four copies of the fraction pieces on page 129. Have your child glue each copy onto cardboard. Then, have her cut out the fraction pieces on three of the copies, keeping the fourth copy intact.

Comments

Fraction pieces allow your child to compare fractions based on their length. Your child can easily see that the fraction 1/2 is larger than the fraction 1/3 by looking at the length of the two fraction pieces. Also, fraction pieces let your child use trial and error to explore the relationships between fractions. For example, if your child puts two 1/2 fraction pieces together, she gets one piece. Just making the fraction pieces teaches your child a lot about fraction concepts.

Fraction Concept Activity 2

Fraction Trains

(age 8 or older)

Materials

Fraction pieces made in Fraction Concept Activity 1

Procedure

Show your child how to make a fraction train with the fraction pieces. Place two 1/3 fraction pieces end to end forming a fraction train to represent the fraction 2/3.

$\dfrac{1}{3}$	$\dfrac{1}{3}$

Have your child use the fraction pieces to make fraction trains for 2/4, 3/4, 2/5, 3/5, 4/5, 2/6, 3/6, 4/6, 5/6, and so on up to 11/12. For each train, ask your child, "How many fraction pieces did you use?" Have her notice that the number of fraction pieces she used is the same number as the top number of the fraction train she made. The top number of a fraction is called the numerator. It represents the number of equal parts in a fraction.

Next, show your child that a fraction train of two 1/2 fraction pieces is the same length as the one piece.

One	
$\dfrac{1}{2}$	$\dfrac{1}{2}$

Have your child use fraction pieces (1/3, 1/4, and so on, up to 1/12) to make trains that are the same length as the one piece. For each train, ask your child, "How many fraction pieces did you use to make the one piece?" Have her notice that the number of fraction pieces she used to make the one piece is the same number as the bottom number of each fraction piece. The bottom number of a fraction is called the denominator. It represents the total number of parts of the whole, the "one," in a fraction.

From *Helping Children with Mathematics, Grades 3–5*, published by GoodYearBooks. Copyright © 1996 James Riley, Marge Eberts, and Peggy Gisler.

Fraction Concept Activity 3

Equivalent Fraction Trains

(age 9 or older)

Materials

Fraction pieces made in Fraction Concept Activity 1
Pencil and paper

Procedure

Equivalent fractions are different fractions that represent the same number. For example, 1/2 = 2/4 = 3/6. In this activity, your child will explore the meaning of equivalent fractions.

Start with the 1/2 fraction piece. Show your child that a train of two 1/4 fraction pieces is the same length as the 1/2 fraction piece.

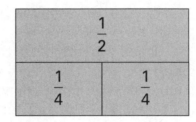

Ask your child to find other trains that are the same length as the 1/2 fraction piece. She should find fraction trains of 3/6, 4/8, 5/10, and 6/12.

Have your child build fraction trains that are the same length as each of these fraction pieces: 1/3, 2/3, 1/4, 3/4, 1/5, 2/5, 3/5, 4/5, 1/6, and 5/6. For the lengths that do not have a fraction piece, have her create the fraction length from 1/3, 1/4, 1/5, and 16 fraction pieces. For example, two 1/3 fraction pieces will make 2/3.

When your child can easily make equivalent fraction trains, have her record the equalities using fraction notation. The fraction trains equivalent to 1/2 would be written as 1/2 = 2/4 = 3/6 = 4/8 = 5/10 = 6/12.

Further Work

After your child understands the equivalent fraction concept, show her that multiplying the numerator and denominator of a fraction by the same number creates an equivalent fraction. For example, 1/2 = 1/2 × 2/2 = 2/4. Have your child find equivalent fractions by using this rule and then verify the result with fraction pieces.

Do not explain this rule to your child too soon. It is important that the proper conceptual development has occurred before parents show children the easy way to find the answer.

Fraction Concept Activity 4

Fraction Concentration

(age 9 or older)

Materials

Make a card for each of the following fractions: 1/2, 2/4, 3/6, 4/8, 5/10, 6/12, 1/3, 2/6, 3/9, 4/12, 2/3, 4/6, 1/4, 2/8, 1/5, 2/10, 2/5, 4/10, 1/6, 2/12, 3/5, 6/10, 4/5, 8/10, 3/4, 6/8, 5/6, 10/12, 6/9, and 8/12

Procedure

Shuffle the fraction cards, and then deal out five rows of six cards facedown. The first player turns over two cards. If they are equivalent fractions, the player puts them in a stack by his side. If not, the cards are returned to the same position, and the next player attempts to find two cards that are equivalent fractions. Whenever a player matches two equivalent fractions, the player can turn over two more cards. Play continues until all the cards have been matched. The winner is the player with the most pairs of equivalent fractions.

Until children become skilled at matching equivalent fractions, they will find it helpful to have the actual fraction pieces or fraction pieces board available to help them find equivalent fractions.

Comments

Remind your child that she can find equivalent fractions by multiplying the numerator and denominator by the same number as shown in Fraction Concept Activity 3.

From *Helping Children with Mathematics, Grades 3–5*, published by GoodYearBooks. Copyright © 1996 James Riley, Marge Eberts, and Peggy Gisler.

Fraction Concept Activity 5

Mixing Fractions

(age 9 or older)

Materials

Fraction pieces
made in Fraction
Concept Activity 1
Pencil and paper

▼

Procedure

A mixed number is a number represented by a whole number and a fraction, like 2 3/4. An improper fraction is a fraction that represents a mixed number or a whole number, like 11/4 or 4/1. In this activity, your child will explore the relationship between mixed numbers and improper fractions.

Have your child make a fraction train consisting of a one fraction piece and a 1/2 fraction piece. This is the mixed number 1 1/2. Then have her make a train with 1/2 fraction pieces that is the same length as the 1 1/2 train. Three 1/2 fraction pieces will be used. The two trains should look like this.

One		$\frac{1}{2}$
$\frac{1}{2}$	$\frac{1}{2}$	$\frac{1}{2}$

Have her write the mixed number and improper fraction as an equality. For example, 1 1/2 = 3/2.

Have your child repeat the activity making fraction trains that represent these mixed numbers: 1 1/3, 1 2/3, 1 1/4, 1 3/4, 1 1/5, 1 2/5, 1 3/5, 1 4/5, 1 1/6, 1 5/6, 1 1/8, 1 3/8, 1 5/8, 1 7/8, 1 1/9, 1 2/9, 1 4/9, 1 5/9, 1 7/9, 1 8/9, 1 1/10, 1 3/10, 1 7/10, and 1 9/10.

Have your child reverse the activity starting with a fraction train that represents an improper fraction, like 5/3, 7/4, and 7/6.

Further Work

After your child has worked Addition of Fractions with Like Denominators (Fraction Activity 1), return to this activity.

A mixed number can be thought of as the addition of fractions with like denominators. For example, 1 2/3 is 1 + 2/3. And, 1 + 3/3. So 1 2/3 = 1 + 2/3 = 3/3 + 2/3 = 5/3. Have your child change the above mixed numbers into improper fractions using this procedure.

Tic-Tac Game Boards

20	6	10
8	12	1
18	4	24

30	5	16
4	12	6
18	2	24

30	2	10
3	12	8
15	6	36

20	4	9
6	12	3
15	5	25

Advanced
Tic-Tac Game Boards

16	10	56
25	63	49
8	18	30

24	35	14
32	64	26
36	6	54

18	12	15
9	72	27
48	28	40

36	45	24
42	81	21
20	12	4

Multiplication Scramble

x	1	2	3	4	5	6	7	8	9
1									
2									
3									
4									
5									
6									
7									
8									
9									

Multipaths

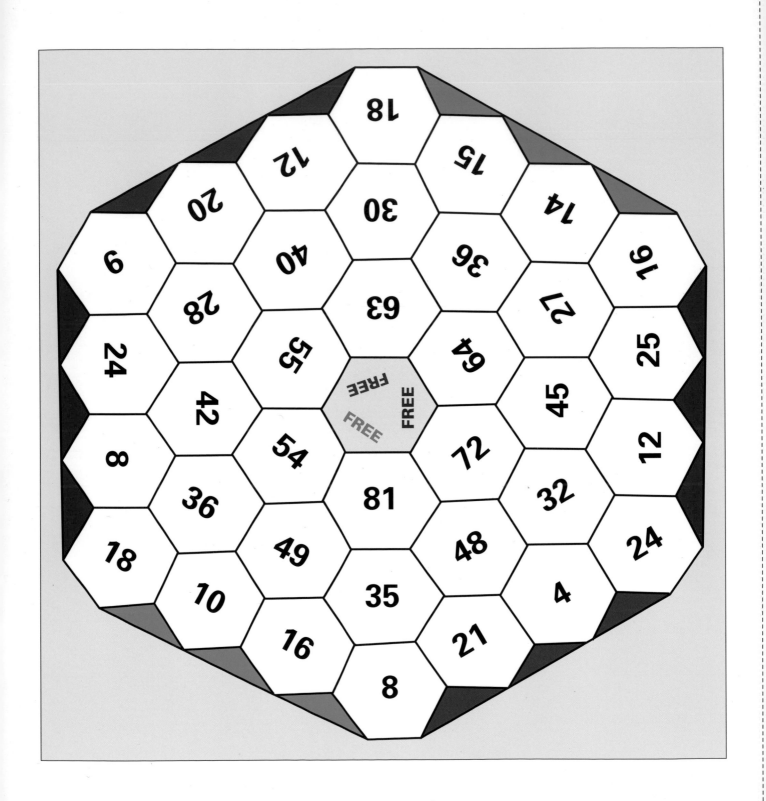

The Addition and Subtraction of Fractions

The addition and subtraction of fractions activities, as with others in the book, concentrate on the development of concepts rather than on rote learning and the memorization of procedures. While children can easily learn to handle fraction operations, they can also be confused about which rule to follow unless they understand the fraction concepts. The use of fraction pieces as models for fractions is continued.

Fraction Activity 1

Addition of Fractions with Like Denominators

(age 9 or older)

From *Helping Children with Mathematics, Grades 3–5*, published by GoodYearBooks. Copyright © 1996 James Riley, Marge Eberts, and Peggy Gisler.

Materials

Fraction pieces
made in Fraction
Concept Activity 1
Pencil and paper
Your child's
mathematics
textbook

Procedure

Find a page in your child's mathematics textbook that has addition of fractions with like denominators problems, such as 2/12 + 3/12. Have your child make fraction trains for each fraction addend.

$\frac{2}{12}$:
| $\frac{1}{12}$ | $\frac{1}{12}$ |

$\frac{3}{12}$:
| $\frac{1}{12}$ | $\frac{1}{12}$ | $\frac{1}{12}$ |

Have her push the two fraction trains together to form one train.

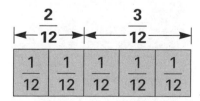

Have her count the number of 1/12 fraction pieces in the combined train. Ask her, "What fraction does the train show?" The combined train represents the fraction 5/12. So 2/12 + 3/12 = 5/12. Have your child write out the addition problem and its sum.

After your child has worked a series of problems, ask her to make up a rule for adding fractions with like denominators. The rule is to add the numerators and use the like denominator.

Have your child rework the addition problems using the rule to find the sums without the fraction pieces.

Comments

This activity should be easy for your child if she has worked through all the fraction activities up to this point. From the prior activities, she has learned all that she needs to know to add fractions with like denominators. This activity just focuses your child's attention on the addition operation.

From *Helping Children with Mathematics, Grades 3–5*, published by GoodYearBooks. Copyright © 1996 James Riley, Marge Eberts, and Peggy Gisler.

Fraction Activity 2

Subtraction of Fractions with Like Denominators

(age 9 or older)

From *Helping Children with Mathematics, Grades 3–5*, published by GoodYearBooks. Copyright © 1996 James Riley, Marge Eberts, and Peggy Gisler.

Materials

Fraction pieces made in Fraction Concept Activity 1

Pencil and paper

Your child's mathematics textbook

Procedure

Find a page in your child's mathematics textbook that has subtraction of fractions with like denominators problems, such as 5/6 – 2/6. Have your child model the problem with fraction trains.

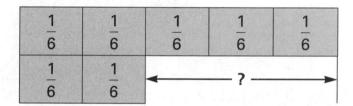

Ask your child, "How many 1/6 fraction pieces must be added to the 2/6 fraction train to be as long as the 5/6 fraction train?" Three 1/6 fraction pieces are needed. So 5/6 – 2/6 = 3/6. Have your child write out the subtraction problem and its difference.

After your child has worked a series of problems, ask her to make up a rule for subtracting fractions with like denominators. The rule is to subtract the numerators and use the like denominator.

Have your child rework the subtraction problems using the rule to find the differences without the fraction pieces.

Comments

The model used to develop the concept of subtraction of fractions is the missing addend model. This model answers the question "How much must be added to the smaller number to equal the larger number?"

From *Helping Children with Mathematics, Grades 3–5*, published by GoodYearBooks. Copyright © 1996 James Riley, Marge Eberts, and Peggy Gisler.

Fraction Activity 3

Addition of Fractions with Unlike Denominators

(age 9 or older)

Procedure

Let's use the fraction addition problem 1/2 + 1/3 as an example of the procedure to use in this activity. Have your child make a fraction train illustrating the problem 1/2 + 1/3.

$\frac{1}{2}$	$\frac{1}{3}$

Point out that to add fractions of unlike denominators, she must find a like denominator before she can add. Have your child make a fraction train with fraction pieces of the same denominator that is the same length as the 1/2 + 1/3 train.

$\frac{1}{2}$			$\frac{1}{3}$	
$\frac{1}{6}$	$\frac{1}{6}$	$\frac{1}{6}$	$\frac{1}{6}$	$\frac{1}{6}$

The new fraction train shows that the original problem can be represented with two equivalent fractions, 1/2 = 3/6 and 1/3 = 2/6. So 1/2 + 1/3 = 3/6 + 2/6 = 5/6. Have your child write out the complete fraction sentence.

Have your child work through the following problems using the same procedure.

1/2 + 2/3, 1/2 + 1/4, 1/2 + 1/6, 1/2 + 3/4, 1/2 + 5/6, 1/4 + 1/3, 1/4 + 2/3,

1/3 + 1/6, 1/3 + 5/6, 2/3 + 3/4, 2/3 + 5/6, 3/4 + 2/3, 1/6 + 1/4, 3/4 + 5/6

For more problems involving addition of fractions with unlike denominators, consult your child's mathematics textbook.

Comments

After completing this activity, have your child return to the Mixing Fractions activity to complete the Further Work section.

Materials

Fraction pieces made in Fraction Concept Activity 1

Pencil and paper

Fraction Activity 4

Subtraction of Fractions with Unlike Denominators

(age 9 and older)

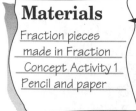

Materials

Fraction pieces
made in Fraction
Concept Activity 1
Pencil and paper

Procedure

Let's use the fraction subtraction problem 2/3 – 1/2 as an example of the procedure to use in this activity. Have your child model the problem with fraction pieces as shown below.

$\frac{1}{3}$	$\frac{1}{3}$
$\frac{1}{2}$	?

Point out to your child that to subtract fractions of unlike denominators, she must find a like denominator before she can subtract. Have your child set up a problem equivalent to 2/3 – 1/2 using fraction pieces of the same denominator.

$\frac{1}{6}$	$\frac{1}{6}$	$\frac{1}{6}$	$\frac{1}{6}$
$\frac{1}{6}$	$\frac{1}{6}$	$\frac{1}{6}$	

Then, have her determine how many 1/6 fraction pieces must be added to the 3/6 fraction train to be as long as the 4/6 fraction train. In this case, one 1/6 fraction piece is needed. So 2/3 – 1/2 = 4/6 – 3/6 = 1/6. Have your child write out the complete fraction sentence.

Have your child work through the following problems using the same procedure.

1/2 – 1/3, 1/3 – 1/4, 2/3 – 1/4, 1/2 – 1/6, 1/3 – 1/6, 2/3 – 1/6, 3/4 – 1/2,

3/4 – 1/3, 3/4 – 2/3, 5/6 – 1/3, 5/6 – 2/3, 5/6 – 1/4, 5/6 – 3/4, 3/4 – 5/12

For more problems involving subtraction of fractions with unlike denominators, consult your child's mathematics textbook.

The Multiplication of Fractions

Multiplying fractions is simple. You just multiply the numerators and then the denominators, and you are done. The rule is easy to learn and remember. However learning and memorizing a mathematical rule is of little value if your child does not fully understand why the rule is being used. The following activities develop the concepts underlying the rule for the multiplication of fractions.

Fraction Multiplication Activity 1

Whole Number Times a Fraction

(age 10 and older)

Procedure

Let's use the fraction multiplication problem 3 x 2/3 as an example of the procedure to use in this activity. Have your child represent the problem 3 x 2/3.

| $\frac{1}{3}$ | $\frac{1}{3}$ | | $\frac{1}{3}$ | $\frac{1}{3}$ | | $\frac{1}{3}$ | $\frac{1}{3}$ |

Have your child count the number of 2/3 fraction pieces she used, in this case, 3. Have her write out the problem and the product 3 x 2/3 = 6/3. Ask her if she can make up a rule for multiplication of whole numbers times fractions.

Have your child work through the following problems using the same procedure.

> 2 x 2/3, 3 x 3/4, 4 x 2/4, 2 x 5/6, 3 x 5/12, 2 x 7/12, 2 x 11/12

For more problems involving multiplication of whole numbers and fractions, consult your child's mathematics textbook.

Comments

The multiplication of a whole number times a fraction is best demonstrated by the repeated addition model for multiplication. For example, the problem 3 x 2/3 is the same as 2/3 + 2/3 + 2/3.

From *Helping Children with Mathematics, Grades 3–5*, published by GoodYearBooks. Copyright © 1996 James Riley, Marge Eberts, and Peggy Gisler.

Fraction Multiplication Activity 2

Fraction Piece Multiplication

(age 10 and older)

Materials

Fraction pieces
    made in Fraction
    Concept Activity 1
Ruler
Pencil and paper
Scissors

Procedure

Let's use the fraction multiplication problem 1/2 x 3/4 to demonstrate the procedure to use in this activity. Have your child represent the second factor, 3/4, with fraction pieces. Then have her cut a strip of paper that is the same length as the $\frac{3}{4}$ fraction train.

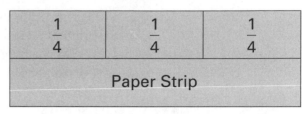

Paper Strip

Folded
Paper Strip

Next, have your child represent the first factor, 1/2, by folding the paper strip in half. Have her find fraction pieces that are the same length as the folded strip.

Have your child write out the problem and the product 1/2 x 3/4 = 3/8.

Have your child work through the following problems using the same procedure.

> 1/2 x 5/6, 1/2 x 3/5, 1/2 x 1/2, 1/2 x 1/3, 1/2 x 1/4,
> 1/2 x 1/5, 1/2 x 1/6, 1/3 x 1/3, 1/3 x 2/3, 1/3 x 1/4

Comments

This activity shows your child that when she multiplies a fraction that is less than 1 times another fraction that is less than 1, the product is less than either of the factors.

Fraction Multiplication Activity 3

Rectangular Multiplication

(age 10 and older)

Materials

Pencil and paper

Scissors

Ruler

Your child's
mathematics
textbook

Procedure

Find a page in your child's mathematics textbook with fraction multiplication problems, like 2/3 x 3/4. Have your child draw a three-inch square on a piece of paper and cut it out. Have her divide the square into three equal horizontal parts to represent the denominator of the first factor, 3.

Then have your child further divide the square into four equal vertical parts to represent the denominator of the second factor, 4. The square is now divided into 12 equal rectangular pieces.

The numerators of the fractions being multiplied are 2 and 3. Have your child shade in rectangular pieces to make a 2 x 3 rectangle in the upper left hand corner of the square.

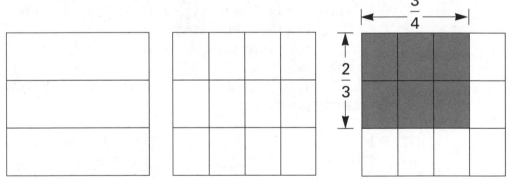

Your child should have shaded 6 of the 12 rectangles in the square. The fraction of shaded rectangles to total rectangles is 6/12. Have your child write out the problem and the product 2/3 x 3/4 = 6/12.

After your child has worked a series of problems, ask her to make up a rule for the multiplication of fractions. The rule is to multiply the numerators and then multiply the denominators.

Have your child rework the fraction multiplication problems using the rule to find the product.

Comments

This activity uses the array model for multiplication. When applied to fractions, the model shows that the product of 2/3 x 3/4 is the area of a rectangle with width of 2/3 and length of 3/4. It may be helpful for your child to review Region I Activity 3 in Chapter 3 to recall how an array model works.

Decimals

Well deal with decimals every day. Grocery scales weigh in decimal pounds. Gasoline is measured in decimal gallons. Prices are listed in decimal dollars. Even grade point averages are figured in decimals. An understanding of decimals is essential if we are to live and cope in our world. The activities in this section concentrate on the use of decimals in everyday life.

Decimal Activity 1

Money, Money, Money

(age 8 and older)

From *Helping Children with Mathematics, Grades 3–5*, published by GoodYearBooks. Copyright © 1996 James Riley, Marge Eberts, and Peggy Gisler.

Materials

Newspapers,
    catalogs,
    advertisement
    flyers
Paper money,
    dimes, and
    pennies
Calculator
A shopping list

Procedure

Ask your child to select priced items from a newspaper or other advertisement that she would like to buy. Have your child count out the exact amount of money needed to buy the item using only pennies, dimes, and paper money. Repeat the activity until your child can easily determine the correct amount of money.

Next, select an item that you would like to buy from the advertisements, but keep it a secret. Count out the money that would be needed to buy that item. Have your child count the money for your item, and try to determine which item you have selected based upon the item's price.

On your next trip to the grocery store have your child accompany you and bring a calculator. As you place each item into the cart, have your child total the cost of the items selected. She may have to get the amount from the pricing information on the shelf.

At the checkout, have your child compare her total with the before-tax total on the cash register receipt.

At home, have your child list the prices of all items purchased in a vertical column, making sure the decimal points are in line. Then have your child add the column of numbers following the procedure used in Addition Activity 4: Drop that Ten.

Further Work

Have your child list in separate columns the prices of all fruits and vegetables, snacks and juices, and meat and fish purchased on your shopping trip. Then she should use her calculator to determine which group of foods cost the most money.

Materials

A calculator
Pencil and paper
Your child's
  mathematics
  textbook

Use Your Calculator

(age 10 and older)

Procedure

Find a set of multiplication problems involving decimals like 34.7 x 12.38 in your child's mathematics textbook. Using a calculator have her find the product ignoring the decimal points. In our problem, she would get 429586.

Ask your child to locate the correct position of the decimal point in the answer. To do this, have her estimate the answer by rounding each factor to the nearest one and multiplying the new factors. For our example, 35 x 12 = 420. Suggest that the decimal be placed in 429586 to get as close as possible to 420 (product of 35 x 12). The decimal point is at 429.586.

After your child has worked through a number of problems, ask her to make up a rule for locating the decimal point in multiplication. It is placed so that the number of digits to the right of the decimal equals the number of decimal places in the factors. For example, there are three decimal places in the problem 34.7 x 12.38, so she should place the decimal three places from the right of the product: 429.586.

Comments

If your child has difficulty understanding the rule for decimals in multiplication, have her work with smaller numbers.

From *Helping Children with Mathematics, Grades 3–5*, published by GoodYearBooks. Copyright © 1996 James Riley, Marge Eberts, and Peggy Gisler.

Percents

Percents are used to represent fraction parts and decimals. The fraction 50/100, the decimal 0.50, as well as 50% represent the same number. Percents are commonly used in everyday life to represent interest rates, tax rates, the amounts of different fibers in clothing, and sales discounts. The first activity demonstrates the extent that percents are used for information in our lives. The second activity requires the use of percents in a problem solving situation using computations.

Percent Activity 1

Percents in the News

(age 10 and older)

Materials

A newspaper
A pen

Procedure

Make sure your child can recognize the percent symbol (%). Explain to your child that percent is Latin and means "out of every 100." So 25% means 25 out of every 100.

Give your child a copy of a newspaper and ask her to find as many examples of percent usage as possible. Every time your child finds such an example have her circle that example in the paper.

Have your child count the total number of references to percents found in the paper. Discuss the meaning of each reference with your child. For example, if a news report states that computer manufacturing orders fell 9 percent last month, that would mean that for every 100 orders received two months ago, only 91 orders were received last month.

Managing Information

Managing information is a necessary skill for children to have in the "information age." Mathematics helps us keep track of and interpret information through graphs, tables, probability studies, and statistics. Children need to have many informal but meaningful experiences in these areas in order to prepare them to deal with information they'll receive later in life.

This chapter includes a number of activities in the areas of graphing, probability, and statistics. Some of the activities will overlap. Even though the main focus of an activity may be a probability or statistics concept, the activity may also involve graphing.

Graphing

Graphing is the presentation of information in a pictorial manner. It is important to know how to read and interpret the different types of graphs because of their frequency in newspapers and magazines. Here we deal with line graphs and a weather map. Bar graphs and a tree graph will be dealt with in the section on probability.

The technique used to work with graphs is a simple one. Children draw graphs based on data they have collected from newspapers, magazines, or books. Then, they are asked questions about the data, answering with the information displayed in their graphs. The following activities acquaint children with the construction and interpretation of line graphs, tables, and a weather map.

Graphing Activity 1

Get a Line on Your Team

(age 9 and older)

Materials

The sports section
 of a newspaper
Grid graph paper
Pencil and paper
Pen and colored
 pencils

Procedure

People who love sports follow their team's progress closely throughout the season. The wins and losses of your child's favorite sports team can be shown on a line graph.

Have your child make a table that tracks the progress of his favorite sports team. For example, if your child's team won the first three games, lost the fourth game, and won the fifth game the table would look like this.

Games Played	Games Won	Ordered Pair
1	1	(1,1)
2	2	(2,2)
3	3	(3,3)
4	3	(4,3)
5	4	(5,4)

As each game is played, have your child fill in the table. From this table, she will make a line graph. The ordered pairs in the table indicate where a dot should be placed on the line graph. The first

From *Helping Children with Mathematics, Grades 3–5*, published by GoodYearBooks. Copyright © 1996 James Riley, Marge Eberts, and Peggy Gisler.

number in the ordered pair is the number of games played and the second number is the number of games won.

On a sheet of grid graph paper, have your child draw horizontal and vertical axis lines along the bottom and left lines of the graph paper. He should label the vertical axis "games won" and the horizontal axis "games played." Then have him number the lines along the horizontal axis and the vertical axis. The grid graph paper should look like this.

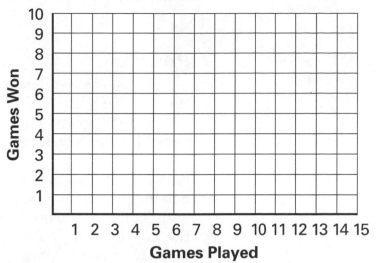

Have your child use the ordered pairs to draw dots on the grid graph paper. For example, the ordered pair, (1,1), tells your child to go across one line and up one line to plot the first dot in our table. Then, connect the dots, dot to dot, as the games are played. The graph of the information in our table would look like this.

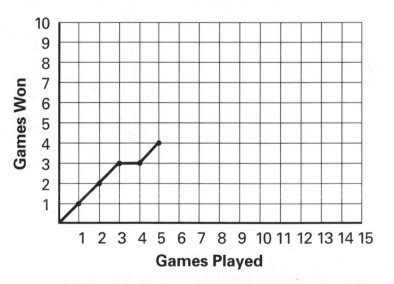

Your child does not have to start with the first game of the season. For example, if his team has won 24 games out of the 37 games played, he should start numbering his graph at 37 along the horizontal axis and 24 along the vertical axis.

Also, your child can chart more than one team on the same graph. Just select a different color for each team and use colored pencils to graph each team's progress.

From *Helping Children with Mathematics, Grades 3–5*, published by GoodYearBooks. Copyright © 1996 James Riley, Marge Eberts, and Peggy Gisler.

Graphing Activity 2

Measure Your Cool

(age 9 and older)

From *Helping Children with Mathematics, Grades 3–5*, published by GoodYearBooks. Copyright © 1996 James Riley, Marge Eberts, and Peggy Gisler.

Materials

An outside
   thermometer
A source for
   weather
   information
Grid graph paper
Colored pencils and
   ruler

Procedure

In this activity, your child can see how good temperature predictions are for your area.

Every day for one week, have your child find the next day's predicted high or low temperature from newspaper or television weather information. He should record this temperature on a graph with a colored pencil. Also, at the same time each day, have your child read an outside thermometer and record the temperature on the same graph with a different colored pencil. Make sure that your child measures the temperature at a time that is likely to be close to the day's high or low. At the end of the week, your child should connect the dots indicating the predicted temperatures to form a line graph. Do the same with the dots indicating the actual temperatures. A line graph of predicted and actual temperatures is shown below.

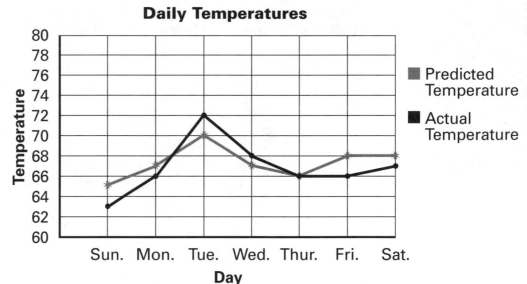

Ask the following questions:

1. Was the predicted temperature exactly the same as the actual temperature for any day?

2. Was the actual temperature usually higher or lower than the predicted temperature?

3. By how many degrees did the actual temperature and predicted temperature differ on each day?

Graphing Activity 3

How's the Weather There?

(age 9 and older)

Materials

A copy of a map of the United States

A daily newspaper

A box of crayons

Pencil and paper

▼

Procedure

This activity looks at how much temperatures across the United States vary. It also shows an interesting way to display mathematical information.

Find a copy of the map of the United States. Have your child find the high and low daily temperatures for each city listed on the map in the weather section of the newspaper. He should record the temperatures in a table like the one below. Using a calculator, have your child find the average temperature for each city, (high + low) / 2. Round to the nearest one.

| City | Temperature | | |
	High	Low	Average
Seattle, WA	69°	50°	60°
Portland, OR	76°	49°	63°
San Francisco, CA	64°	51°	58°

Have your child show the average temperature of each city across the United States by coloring in circles next to each city on the map according to this key:

Average Temperature	Color
80°+	Red
60°–79°	Yellow
40°–59°	Green
39°–	Blue

Ask the following questions:

1. What average temperature range occurred most often across the United States?

2. What average temperature range occurred least often across the United States?

3. What areas of the United States have the highest average temperature? the lowest?

4. How does the average temperature vary across the United States?

Probability

Probability is the mathematics of prediction. When there is more than one possible outcome of an event, probability tells you the likelihood that a certain outcome will occur. Probability is used to predict your chance of winning the lottery. It is also used in complicated computer models that predict anything from next week's weather to next year's economy.

Some probability models are developed by actually observing the outcomes of an experiment, such as predicting the outcomes of tossing a coin 100 times by actually tossing the coin 100 times. Other probability models are developed from a logical and mathematical analysis of possible outcomes. In this case, such an analysis would determine that heads should appear half the time in 100 coin tosses. The following activities will introduce your child to both kinds of probability models.

Probability Activity 1

Differences Among Dice

(age 9 and older)

Materials
A pair of dice
Pencil and paper

Procedure

This activity looks at two probability models to answer the question: What difference is most likely to show up when you roll a pair of dice and compute the difference between the number of dots on the top faces of each die? For example, if a 6 and a 2 are rolled, the difference is 4.

1. Experiment Model

Have your child roll the dice 36 times and find the difference between the number of dots on the top faces of the dice each time. He should make a tally of the number of times each possible difference occurs. Then have him record the results in a graph like the one on page 93.

From *Helping Children with Mathematics, Grades 3–5*, published by GoodYearBooks. Copyright © 1996 James Riley, Marge Eberts, and Peggy Gisler.

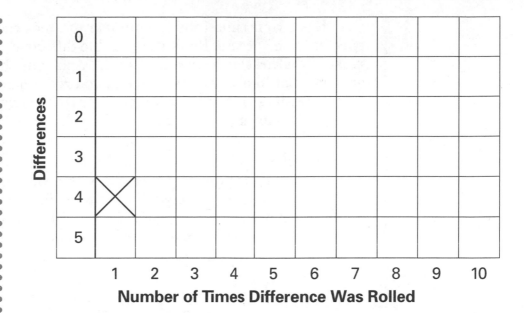

Differences	1	2	3	4	5	6	7	8	9	10
0										
1										
2										
3										
4	✕									
5										

Number of Times Difference Was Rolled

Ask your child to rank the differences shown on the graph from most often (1st) to least often (6th).

Repeat the experiment three more times. Does the difference ranking change very much between the experiments?

Total the number of times each difference occurs for all the times the dice are rolled. Answer the question: What difference is most likely to show up when you roll a pair of dice?

2. Analysis of Possible Outcomes Model

Have your child construct a table that shows all the possible difference outcomes from a roll of a pair of dice. Your child should compute the differences to fill in the table.

First Die	1	2	3	4	5	6
6						
5						
4						
3	2					
2	1					
1	0			3		

Second Die

Have your child tally the number of times each possible difference outcome occurs. Rank the possible difference outcomes from most often (first) to least often (sixth). Ask your child, "What difference is most likely to show up when you roll a pair of dice?"

How does this answer compare with the answer obtained using the experiment model?

Comments

Both models provide your child with a way to predict the outcome of an event. They only tell the probability of an outcome occurring, not what the actual outcome will be. Knowing the likelihood of a certain outcome occurring can help your child make decisions about events in the future.

From *Helping Children with Mathematics, Grades 3–5*, published by GoodYearBooks. Copyright © 1996 James Riley, Marge Eberts, and Peggy Gisler.

Probability Activity 2

What's for Dinner, Chicken or Fish?

(age 10 or older)

▼

Procedure

Have your child help you decide what's for dinner: chicken or fish. The dinner choice will depend on the outcomes of a roll of a die and a draw from a bag.

Have him place 3 red blocks and 2 green blocks in a bag labeled I, and 2 red blocks and 3 green blocks in a bag labeled II. Have your child roll a die. If the die shows 1 dot or 2 dots on the top face, have him select a block from Bag I without looking. Otherwise, he should select a block from Bag II. If he selects a red block from either bag, dinner will be chicken; if it's a green block, dinner will be fish.

Before beginning the dinner choice process, have your child try to predict whether fish or chicken is the most likely result. Have her plot the possible outcomes of the dinner choice process in a tree graph. An example of one tree graph your child could make is shown below.

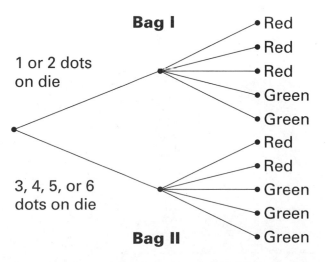

Bag I

1 or 2 dots
on die

• Red
• Red
• Red
• Green
• Green

• Red
• Red
• Green
• Green
• Green

3, 4, 5, or 6
dots on die

Bag II

Ask the following questions:

1. What bag are you most likely to draw from?

2. What colored block are you most likely to draw from the bag in question 1?

3. What dinner will most likely be chosen?

Have your child perform the dinner choice process—rolling a die and drawing from a bag. Have him compare the results with the pre-choice prediction. Repeat the process 15 times. How many times would dinner have been chicken?

Comments

This activity uses a tree graph to model the possible dinner choice outcomes. A tree graph is one of the best ways to help your child understand a probability decision that depends upon more than one event. In our example, the dinner choice depended upon the roll of a die and the colored block drawn from a bag. The model lets your child see easily and clearly all the possible outcomes of each event and how they relate to each other.

From *Helping Children with Mathematics, Grades 3–5*, published by GoodYearBooks. Copyright © 1996 James Riley, Marge Eberts, and Peggy Gisler.

Statistics

Statistics are used to describe complex sets of information. We try to reduce vast amounts of information to one or two measures. The age range of students in elementary school, the average annual rainfall in the Midwest, the median income for people in the United States, and the most often ordered food at a snack bar are all examples of using one measure to describe a very complex situation. Measures like these help us make decisions in our lives.

The following activities explore the concepts of range, mean, median, and mode.

Statistics Activity 1

How Long Is a Word?

(age 10 and older)

Materials
A newspaper or
  magazine
Pencil and paper
A calculator

Procedure

Have your child select an article from a newspaper or magazine. Have him count the number of letters in each word of the first few paragraphs. Record the number of letters in a bar graph. For example, the length of each word in the first sentence of this chapter on page 87 would look like this:

Word Length	Number of Words						
1	☒						
2	☒	☒					
3	☒	☒					
4	☒						
5	☒						
6							
7							
8	☒	☒					
9	☒						
10							
11	☒	☒					
12							

Using the information in the bar graph and a calculator, have your child find the following statistical measures:

1. Range

The range is the difference between the greatest number and least number. Have your child subtract the number of letters in the least word from the number of letters in the greatest word in the article to determine the range. For example, in the first sentence of this chapter, the range of word length is 11 letters – 1 letter = 10 letters.

2. Mean

The mean is the average. For each word length in the article, have him multiply the number of words of that length by the number of letters in each word. If there were 15 words that were 8 letters long, your child would multiply 15 x 8 = 120. Total these products and divide their sum by the total number of words in the article to find the mean. For example, in the first sentence of this chapter the total of the products, 77, divided by the total number of words, 14, is the mean word length of 5.5 letters.

3. Median

The median is the middle number where half the numbers are above and half the numbers are below. If all the words in the article were placed in order from the shortest to the longest, the number in the middle would represent the median. Have your child divide the total number of words in the article by two. Then, have your child start counting the number of words from the shortest to the longest until he reaches the number that resulted from the division. The word length he is at will be the median. For example, in the first sentence of this chapter, 14 total words divided by 2 equals 7, and starting at the shortest word, count 7 marks to find the median. But notice that to have half the numbers below and half the numbers above, the middle is the 3 and 4 word lengths. In this case, the median would be between 3 and 4 word lengths.

4. Mode

The mode is the most frequent outcome. Have your child find the most often used word length in his article to determine the mode. For example, in the first sentence of this chapter the modes are 2 and 3 because there are three words that contain two letters and three words that contain three letters.

From *Helping Children with Mathematics, Grades 3–5,* published by GoodYearBooks. Copyright © 1996 James Riley, Marge Eberts, and Peggy Gisler.

Statistics Activity 2

Who's Talking Now?

(age 10 and older)

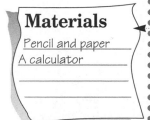

Materials

Pencil and paper
A calculator

Procedure

Place a table like the one below next to each telephone in your home. Establish a family rule that anyone using the telephone during a week must record their telephone use time in the table.

Family Member	Starting Time	Stopping Time	Total Time in Minutes
Mom	7:00	7:15	15
Scott	8:10	8:25	15

Have your child determine the following from the table:

1. What is the range of time spent on phone calls?

2. What is the average amount of time (mean) the family spends on phone calls?

3. Which family member spends the least/most time on the phone?

4. What is the median time spent on the phone? Arrange the phone calls from least amount of time to greatest amount of time. Find the middle number on the list.

5. Which time interval has the most phone calls? Group the calls in the following intervals: 0 to 5 minutes, 6 to 15 minutes, 16 to 30 minutes, 31 to 45 minutes, 46 to 60 minutes, and over 60 minutes.

Comments

Refer back to Statistics Activity 1, if your child is not clear on the definition of and procedure for determining the range, mean, median, and mode.

Materials

The business
   section of a
   newspaper
Pencil and paper
A calculator

The A&G 5 Stock Average

(age 10 or older)

Procedure

Alice and George have created their own measure of the stock market's performance, called the A&G 5 Stock Average. They developed their measure by choosing stocks of companies that were important to them. The A&G 5 contains: McDonald's (McDonld), Coca-Cola (CocaCl), Toys R Us (ToyRU), Reebok (Reebok), and Walt Disney (Disney).

Alice and George compute the A&G 5 daily. In the business section of their newspaper, they find the closing price (last) for each stock and then find the average of the five stocks. This is the A&G 5 Stock Average. Each day they compare that day's average with the previous day's average. If the A&G 5 Stock Average is higher, then they declare that the stock market was up; if it is lower, the stock market was down.

Have your child use the A&G 5 Stock Average or create his own four or five stock average. For a one-week period, have your child follow the A&G 5 or his own stock average. Also, have your child follow the S&P 500 Index (Standard & Poor's) in the same manner. This index tracks the movement of 500 stocks. The S&P 500 Index is used as one measure of the average performance of the stock market.

Have your child compare the A&G 5 Stock Average to the S&P 500. Did they measure the performance of the stock market in the same way, that is up, down, unchanged? Don't worry about the amount of change, just focus on the direction of change. At the end of the week, rate how good a measure the A&G 5 Stock Average is of the stock market compared to the S&P 500 Index. Use a calculator to help with the calculations.

The table below follows the A&G 5 and S&P 500 for part of a week. Your child should make a similar table to this one.

Day	A&G 5	Change	S&P 500	Change	A&G 5 vs S&P 500
Tuesday	41.700	—	454.81	—	—
Wednesday	41.975	↑0.275	456.34	↑1.53	Agree ↑
Thursday	41.925	↑0.050	457.06	↓0.72	Disagree

Note: The business section in the newspaper gives stock information for the previous day.

From *Helping Children with Mathematics, Grades 3–5*, published by GoodYearBooks. Copyright © 1996 James Riley, Marge Eberts, and Peggy Gisler.

## Chapter 5

Geometry and Measurement

Until recently, geometry in elementary school has been limited to learning the names of certain geometric shapes and the basic ideas of measurement. Now a wide range of topics is covered in third, fourth, and fifth grades to help children gain insight into and appreciation of this fascinating topic. When children meet these ideas again in high school, they will recognize them as old friends rather than scary strangers.

Measurement and geometry are closely related as measurement is used to quantify geometric shapes. Beyond this, measurement is used in countless daily activities from telling time to preparing meals. No matter what we measure, we are always dealing with a unit of measure whether it is feet, meters, minutes, or gallons.

Geometry Activities

Geometry literally means measurement of the Earth. At first, geometry was the mathematics of measuring land. It later turned into the study of shapes and their properties which is part of the geometry curriculum in both elementary and high school. Much of today's geometry is so far from the original ideas that early specialists in geometry would not recognize it. This is the geometry that is being used to design closets and computer circuits, make organization charts, and navigate spaceships and is part of the geometry your children will be learning.

Young children take the first steps towards understanding geometry by exploring the shapes or objects in their environment. In third, fourth, and fifth grades, they are introduced to the properties of shapes and measures of area and volume. We've included many hands-on activities in this chapter to give your children an opportunity to develop these skills through drawing, cutting, folding, flipping, and rotating geometric shapes. We have also included activities that introduce them to other ways in which geometry is currently being used whether it is by city planners, sociologists, or computer designers.

Many of the terms in this chapter will be new to your children— some may even be new to you. Keep working on an activity until all of the terms have been mastered, as knowing the vocabulary plays a large role in understanding geometry.

A Different Geometry

A Different Geometry introduces your child to areas of geometry which may be unfamiliar to you. The first activity explores graph theory, which is the study of networks such as the lines of communication in a corporation or the most efficient routes for delivering newspapers and mail. The remaining activities in this section give your children a chance to work with tessellations. A tessellation is the covering of a flat surface with geometric shapes in a repeating pattern with no gaps or overlaps. The tessellation activities develop your child's understanding of spatial relationships—the sense of shapes and how they relate to each other. They also produce beautiful artwork to display in your home.

A D i f f e r e n t G e o m e t r y A c t i v i t y 1

Take a Walk Through Konigsberg

(age 10 or older)

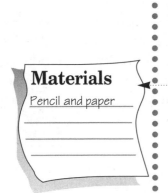

Materials

Pencil and paper

Procedure

The city of Konigsberg, Germany, is located on a river. There are two islands in the center of the river, and a number of bridges connect the islands with the riverbanks. A game developed in which the citizens of Konigsberg tried to see if it was possible to leave one's home on a walk, cross each bridge only once, and return home. The map of the islands and bridges is shown on page 103. A walk through Konigsberg is a network problem. Here are some more network problems.

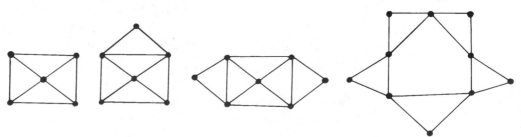

From *Helping Children with Mathematics, Grades 3–5*, published by GoodYearBooks. Copyright © 1996 James Riley, Marge Eberts, and Peggy Gisler.

Have your child try to trace two different paths in each of the networks. For the first path, she must use every line only once but does not have to end up where she started. For the second path, she must use every line only once and also end up where she started.

The dots in each network are called vertices, and the lines connecting the dots are called edges. Each vertex is said to be either odd or even. A vertex is odd if an odd number of edges come into it. A vertex is even if an even number of edges come into it.

Copy the map of Konigsberg onto a piece of paper. Have your child see if she can take a walk through Konigsberg that allows her to cross each bridge only once and end up where she started.

After your child has tried to solve Konigsberg and the other network problems for awhile, introduce her to the discovery of Leonhard Euler, a Swiss mathematician. Euler discovered that a path could be found that uses each edge only once but does not end up where you started if there are two or less odd vertices in the network. Further, a path could be found that uses each edge only once and ends up where you started if, and only if, all the vertices in the network are even.

In each network, have your child determine whether a vertex is odd or even and find a total for the number of odd and the number of even vertices. Then using Euler's discovery, have her see if paths can be found in the following networks:

Network 1: 4 odd vertices and 1 even vertex

No paths can be found.

Network 2: 2 odd vertices and 4 even vertices

A path can be found that uses each edge only once, but you must start at one of the odd vertices and end up at the other one.

Network 3: 7 even vertices

A path can be found that uses each edge only once and ends up where you started.

Network 4: 10 even vertices

A path can be found that uses each edge only once and ends up where you started.

Konigsberg: 4 odd vertices and 5 even vertices

To find this, turn the picture of Konigsberg into a network by drawing lines and making intersection points. A walk through Konigsberg crossing every bridge only once and returning back home is impossible.

If your child has not already discovered the paths that can be found in the networks, have her try again.

Comments

Graph Theory is concerned with how elements relate to each other. In this activity, the solution of the network problems depends on the relationship between the edges and vertices, the elements.

From *Helping Children with Mathematics, Grades 3–5*, published by GoodYearBooks. Copyright © 1996 James Riley, Marge Eberts, and Peggy Gisler.

From *Helping Children with Mathematics, Grades 3–5,* published by GoodYearBooks. Copyright © 1996 James Riley, Marge Eberts, and Peggy Gisler.

A Different Geometry Activity 2

Have You Got It Covered?

(ages 8 and older)

Materials

<u>Copy of shapes for</u>
<u>tessellations</u>
<u>(see page 130)</u>
<u>Construction paper</u>
<u>Pencil and ruler</u>
<u>Scissors</u>
<u>Glue</u>

Procedure

Your child is going to construct each tessellation below so that the pattern covers an entire sheet of paper without gaps or overlaps. This teaches your child to recognize shapes in different positions.

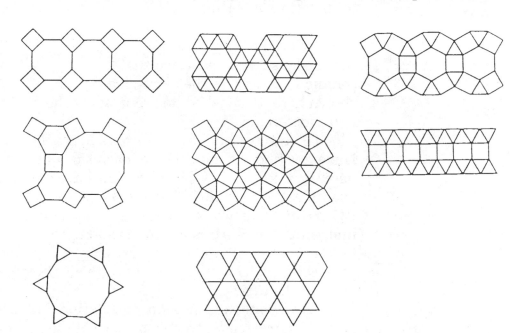

Have your child trace the geometric shapes for the tessellations onto construction paper. She should then cut out the shapes using a different color of paper for each geometric shape. Your child should make enough of each shape to create all of the tessellations. If your child folds the construction paper so that she is cutting through several layers at a time, she can make the shapes faster. Also, you can duplicate the geometric shapes onto colored paper.

Have your child glue the geometric shapes onto construction paper to make each one of the tessellations.

With each tessellation, have your child trace with her finger all of the shapes that circle one vertex and name the shapes. If your child does not know the name of a shape, have her identify it as a ___-sided figure. Notice that in the first tessellation, each vertex is circled by a square, octagon, and octagon. The number of sides in each geometric shape that forms a vertex is used to name the tessellation. Therefore, the first tessellation is identified as 4.8.8. Have your child name all of the tessellations in this manner.

From *Helping Children with Mathematics, Grades 3–5*, published by GoodYearBooks. Copyright © 1996 James Riley, Marge Eberts, and Peggy Gisler.

A Different Geometry Activity 3

Creating Vertex Patterns

(age 8 and older)

Materials

Copy of tessellations (see pages 130-35)

Paper

Pencil and pen

Box of crayons

Ruler

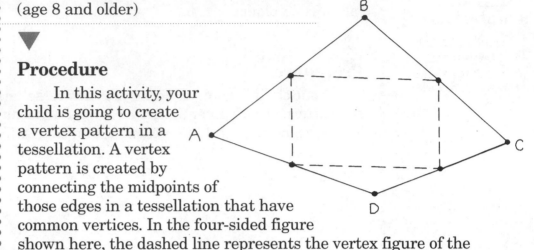

Procedure

In this activity, your child is going to create a vertex pattern in a tessellation. A vertex pattern is created by connecting the midpoints of those edges in a tessellation that have common vertices. In the four-sided figure shown here, the dashed line represents the vertex figure of the four-sided figure.

Have your child draw figure ABCD above on a piece of paper. Have her find the midpoints of each side of the figure. She should connect the midpoints of the edges that have a common vertex. For example, the midpoint of edge AB is connected to the midpoint of edge BC because the two edges have B as a common vertex. However, the midpoint of edge AB is not connected to the midpoint of edge DC because edges AB and DC do not share a common vertex. Make sure your child understands how to create a vertex figure before continuing on with the activity.

Have your child select a tessellation. Make a photocopy of it. Have her draw in the vertex pattern of the photocopied tessellation. Have her use a pencil in case she makes errors. When the vertex pattern is correctly drawn, it can be traced over with a pen. Let your child crayon in the design.

In the following drawing, the dashed lines show the vertex pattern of a 3.3.3.4.4 tessellation.

Have your child work through the complete set of tessellations, drawing in the vertex patterns and coloring them.

Comments

By drawing a vertex pattern, children are generating more complex tessellations from tessellations as new shapes are created. Wallpaper patterns and fabric designs are often made in this way.

Drawing, Cutting, and Folding

I n the past, most students were not introduced to many geometric ideas until they studied the subject in high school. Now most of the concepts of high school geometry are being introduced much earlier. The activities in this section use drawing, cutting, and folding to investigate some ideas of traditional high school geometry.

Drawing, Cutting, and Folding Activity 1

Getting the Angle on Polygons

(age 10 and older)

From *Helping Children with Mathematics, Grades 3–5*, published by GoodYearBooks. Copyright © 1996 James Riley, Marge Eberts, and Peggy Gisler.

Materials

Ruler
Pencil and paper
Scissors
Compass
Protractor
Cellophane tape
Calculator
_____
_____
_____
_____

Procedure

This activity helps your child develop the formula to find the sum of the angle measures of polygons (a closed figure made up of sides with line segments). Triangles and quadrilaterals are examples of polygons.

Angles of a Triangle

Have your child draw a triangle, a three-sided figure, with a pencil and ruler. Using the compass, she should mark off three equal cutting lines at the corners. Then, have her cut off the vertex angles (corners) of the triangle and tape the cut vertices together. These steps are illustrated below.

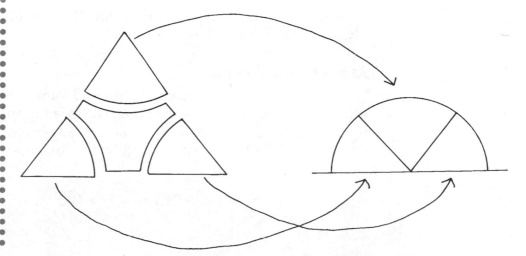

Notice that the angles form a straight line. The sum of the angles of any triangle is a straight line.

Have your child repeat the activity using different shaped and sized triangles. She will find that the sum of the angles will always form a straight line, 180°.

Angles of a Quadrilateral

Have your child follow the same steps as for the triangle to determine the sum of the angles of a quadrilateral (a four-sided figure).

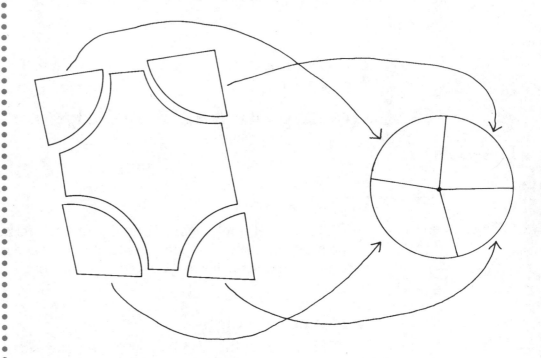

Notice that the angles form a complete circle. The sum of the angles of any quadrilateral is a full circle.

Have your child repeat the activity using different-shaped and sized quadrilaterals. She will find that the sum of the angles will always form a circle, 360°.

Angles of a Polygon

In the first two exercises, your child found the sum of the vertex angles of three- and four-sided figures. This finding can be generalized to apply to all polygons. The sum of the vertex angle measures of a polygon (S) with n sides is given by the formula:

$$S = (n - 2) \times 180°$$

From *Helping Children with Mathematics, Grades 3–5*, published by GoodYearBooks. Copyright © 1996 James Riley, Marge Eberts, and Peggy Gisler.

Have your child discover this formula. For each number of sides, *n*, in the table below, have your child draw an n-sided polygon with a pencil and ruler. Using the protractor, she should measure the vertex angles of the drawn polygon. Write the measurements inside each vertex angle. Have her add the vertex angle measurements with a calculator and record the result in the table. Next, have your child solve the above formula for that n-sided polygon. Have her compare the sum she found with the one the formula finds. They should be close.

n	*S*	Your Sum
3	180°	
4	360°	
5	540°	
6	720°	
7	900°	
8	1,080°	

From *Helping Children with Mathematics, Grades 3–5*, published by GoodYearBooks. Copyright © 1996 James Riley, Marge Eberts, and Peggy Gisler.

From *Helping Children with Mathematics, Grades 3–5*, published by GoodYearBooks. Copyright © 1996 James Riley, Marge Eberts, and Peggy Gisler.

Drawing, Cutting, and Folding Activity 2

Getting the Angle on Circles

(age 9 and older)

Materials

Compass
Pencil and paper
Ruler
Scissors

Procedure

This activity demonstrates the relationship between the central angle and an inscribed angle of a circle. Before your child begins, you should talk about what the central angles and inscribed angles of a circle are. A central angle of a circle is an angle whose vertex is the center of the circle. The figure at the right shows the central angle of a circle.

An inscribed angle of a circle is an angle formed by joining any point on the circle's circumference (the distance around a circle) with any two other points on a circle. The figure at the right shows an inscribed angle of a circle.

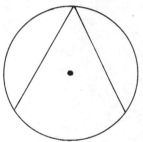

The relationship between a central angle and an inscribed angle of a circle is that the central angle is twice the measure of its inscribed angle.

Have your child find this relationship by using a compass to draw a circle around a center mark. Then she should use a ruler to draw in a central angle and its inscribed angle. The central angle is cut out and folded, and is fit into the inscribed angle. The folded central angle will fit perfectly inside the inscribed angle. Have your child repeat the exercise a number of times using different-sized central and inscribed angles.

Drawing, Cutting, and Folding
Activity 3

The Idea Pythagoras Stole

(age 9 and older)

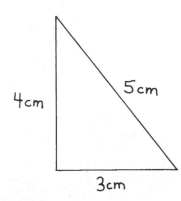

Procedure

Have your child draw a right triangle with sides of 3 centimeters (cm), 4 cm, and 5 cm. She can use the corner of a sheet of paper to make the right angle of the triangle. The 3 cm and 4 cm sides of the triangle with the right angle are called the legs. The 5 cm side opposite the right angle is called the hypotenuse.

Next, have your child make three square pieces of paper. The first square should have sides equal to the length of one of the legs. The second square should have sides equal to the length of the other leg. And, the third square should have sides equal to the length of the hypotenuse. She should place these squares along the sides of the triangle as shown below.

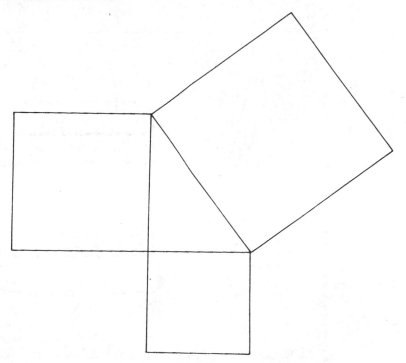

Have your child take one square from a leg side and glue it in the square of the hypotenuse. Then, have her cut the square of the other leg into rectangular pieces to fill the remaining area of the hypotenuse square. All the paper from the leg squares will be used, and no part of the hypotenuse square will be left uncovered. The cutting and pasting of the squares of our right triangle might look like the following.

Point out to your child that the sum of the two leg squares of a right triangle is equal to the square of the hypotenuse as seen above. This is called the Pythagorean Theorem. In our example,

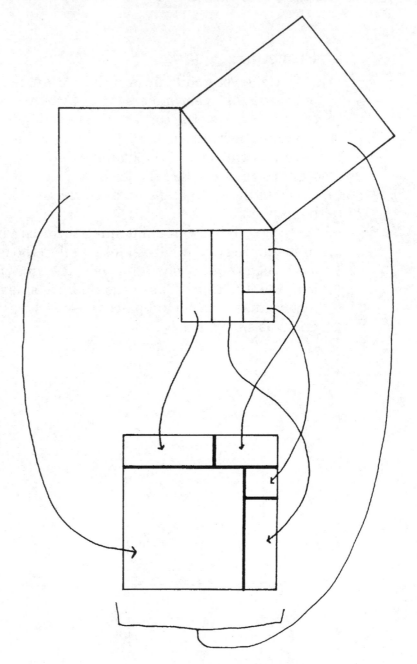

the squares of the legs are 3 x 3 = 9 and 4 x 4 = 16 and the square of the hypotenuse is 5 x 5 = 25. The sum of the two leg squares is 9 + 16 = 25.

From *Helping Children with Mathematics, Grades 3–5,* published by GoodYearBooks. Copyright © 1996 James Riley, Marge Eberts, and Peggy Gisler.

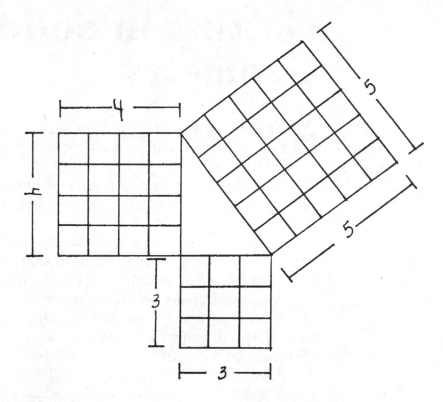

Repeat the activity using other right triangles to prove the Pythagorean Theorem. Don't worry about having your child mathematically solve the theorem. We are only concerned with developing the concept.

Comments

The idea for the Pythagorean Theorem is at least 4,000 years old. Pythagoras lived about 2,500 years ago. While he did not discover the idea, he did prove it to be true.

The Pythagorean Theorem has wide application in mathematics. Much of the mathematical subject called trigonometry is based upon this one idea. There are dozens of proofs of this theorem, including one presented by James Garfield several years before he became the twentieth president of the United States.

Getting in Solid with Geometry

Solid geometry deals with three-dimensional figures. In this section, your child will be working with regular and semiregular geometric solids.

The five regular solids are formed by regular polygons. A regular polygon has all sides equal and all corner angles equal. More than 2,000 years ago, Greek mathematicians believed that these solids held the secret to the structure of all things in the universe. This is not true, of course, but the mathematics that has grown out of these findings is still used by scientists in the study of molecular structure.

The semiregular solids are constructed with two or more different regular polygons. A soccer ball is an example of a semiregular solid. The ball's surface is covered with pentagons and hexagons. Semiregular solids are used to describe chemical compounds.

Geometric solids with polygonal faces are called polyhedra. *Polyhedra* comes from two Greek words, *poly* meaning many and *hedra* meaning faces. For example, an octahedron is a solid with eight triangles for faces.

Solid Geometry Activity 1

The Regular Solids

(age 10 and older)

Materials

Patterns for 5
regular solids (see
pages 136–38)
Cardboard
Pencil
Scissors
Craft glue

▼

Procedure

In this activity, your child will make models of the five regular solids. This is a lengthy activity and may take several days to complete. Your child will construct a cube first because its shape is familiar to everybody, and it is the easiest to make. Then your child will make the other regular solid models following the steps used to make the cube.

The Cube

The cube has six squares as its faces. Each vertex (corner) is formed by three squares.

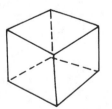

From *Helping Children with Mathematics, Grades 3–5*, published by GoodYearBooks. Copyright © 1996 James Riley, Marge Eberts, and Peggy Gisler.

Have your child make a cube following these steps:

1. Trace the cube pattern onto the cardboard.

2. Cut around the outline of the pattern, including tabs.

3. Fold the cardboard as indicated on the pattern.

4. Use the tabs to glue the sides together to form the cube.

The Tetrahedron

The tetrahedron has four triangles as its faces. Each vertex is formed by three triangles.

The Octahedron

The octahedron has eight triangles as its faces. Each vertex is formed by four triangles.

The Dodecahedron

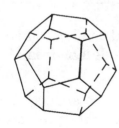

The dodecahedron has 12 regular pentagons (five-sided figures) as its faces. Each vertex is formed by three pentagons.

The Icosahedron

The icosahedron has 20 regular triangles as its faces. Each vertex is formed by five triangles.

Further Work

Have your child use the regular solids she constructed to determine the number of faces, vertices, and edges for each solid. The face of a solid is the flat surface. The vertices of a solid are the corners. The edge of a solid is where two faces meet. The edge connects the vertices. In the following drawing, edge **e** is where face **a** meets face **b** and vertex **c** and vertex **d** are connected.

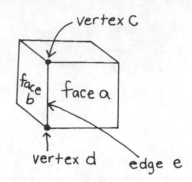

Your child should make her own chart to record this information. The correct numbers for each figure are as follows.

Figures	Faces	Vertices	Edges
Tetrahedron	4 triangles	4	6
Cube	6 squares	8	12
Octahedron	8 triangles	6	12
Dodecahedron	12 pentagons	20	30
Icosahedron	20 triangles	12	30

Have your child study the results and see if she can make any discoveries. Some of the things your child may notice are:

1. The number of edges found in both the cube and octahedron is 12. Likewise, the number of edges in both the dodecahedron and the icosahedron is the same.

2. The number of faces and vertices in the cube and octahedron are reversed. The same is true for the dodecahedron and the icosahedron.

3. The number of faces + the number of vertices = the number of edges + 2. This is called Euler's Relation, and it holds for all solid figures. The relation is named after Leonhard Euler, who discovered this idea and was also the creator of Graph Theory.

From *Helping Children with Mathematics, Grades 3–5*, published by GoodYearBooks. Copyright © 1996 James Riley, Marge Eberts, and Peggy Gisler.

Measurement Activities

Measurement is one of the oldest skills. It was just as important to the ancient world as it is to all of us today. Measurements in the past were made with nonstandard units like a king's foot or the span of a hand. Now we use standard units of measurements such as inches, pints, or minutes. Children need to become familiar with these units, understand the relationships between them, and know how to use them in making measurements.

We introduce your child to the concept of measuring area first; then we progress to the measurement of volume and time. In the activities, we include standard units of measure that are used every day as well as some units that are less familiar to children.

Area Measurement

Area is the measure of the surface inside a shape. It's the carpet that covers the living room floor and the bottom of a fish tank. Children determine the area of a shape by using the appropriate formula for that shape. The activities in this section concentrate on their learning how to develop formulas for finding the area of several geometric shapes. Many of these formulas are related to each other. If children understand the relationship between the formulas, they will be able to recall the appropriate formula easily when they need to use it. The basic formula for the area of a rectangle is considered first. The other formulas for several geometric shapes will be derived from this formula.

Area Measurement Activity 1

Playing with Cards

(age 8 and older)

Materials

Deck(s) of playing cards

Procedure

Have your child lay out playing cards covering the coffee table without overlapping or leaving gaps. Ask your child to count the number of playing cards covering the table. Show her that the number of playing cards needed to cover a rectangular surface, the coffee table, is equal to the product of the number of rows of cards (length) multiplied by the number of columns of cards (width). This is the formula for the area of a rectangle.

$$\text{Area} = \text{Length} \times \text{Width}$$

Repeat the activity, asking your child to find areas of other rectangular surfaces like a kitchen cutting board, a desktop, a newspaper page, a game board, and a pillowcase. After she has measured a number of areas, ask her to compare the areas of the different items. Does the newspaper page have a larger area than the pillowcase?

Comments

In this activity, your child is simply creating a block array model of multiplication which he learned in Region I Activity 3: Arrays of Blocks. Here, playing cards are the blocks. Your child should review the earlier activity before doing this one.

From *Helping Children with Mathematics, Grades 3–5*, published by GoodYearBooks. Copyright © 1996 James Riley, Marge Eberts, and Peggy Gisler.

Materials

Pencil and paper
Scissors
Glue or cellophane
   tape
Ruler

Area Measurement Activity 2

Making Secret Formulas

(age 9 and older)

Procedure

In this activity, your child will change several geometric shapes into other shapes in order to derive area formulas.

1. Area of a Parallelogram

A parallelogram is a four-sided figure with its opposite sides parallel. The figure below is an example of a parallelogram.

A parallelogram can be changed into a rectangle. To do this, have your child draw two same-sized parallelograms using a ruler. Cut out the parallelograms. With one of them, cut off an end and move that end to form a rectangle as illustrated at the right. Tape or glue the newly formed rectangle onto a piece of paper.

Next, have your child measure the length and the width of the newly formed rectangle. Have her determine the area of the rectangle using the formula learned in Area Measurement Activity 1.

Now, have your child measure the dimensions of the uncut parallelogram. The length of a parallelogram is called the base. The distance between the other two parallel sides is called the altitude. Determine the area of the parallelogram by multiplying the length of the base times the altitude.

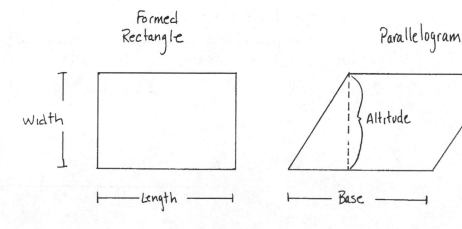

Point out to your child that since the rectangle was made from the parallelogram, their areas are the same. Have your child confirm this by comparing the area she found for the rectangle with the area of the parallelogram.

The formula to find the area of a rectangle will also give you the area of a parallelogram. Only the names in the formula have been changed.

Rectangle:	Area = Length x Width
Parallelogram:	Area = Base x Altitude

2. Area of a Triangle

Every triangle is one-half of a parallelogram. To observe this, have your child draw two parallelograms using a ruler. She should cut out one of the parallelograms, and then cut it in half along a diagonal so she can see the relationship between a triangle and a parallelogram.

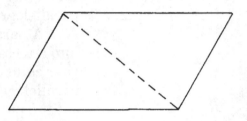

Ask your child to measure the length of the base and the altitude of the uncut parallelogram and then determine its area. Point out to your child that since the triangle is one-half of the parallelogram, then the triangle's area will be one-half the area of the parallelogram.

Parallelogram:	Area = Base x Altitude
Triangle:	Area = 1/2 x Base x Altitude

Have your child determine the area of the triangle and notice this area is one-half the area of the parallelogram.

3. Area of a Trapezoid

A trapezoid is a four-sided figure with two parallel sides. The figure below is an example of a trapezoid.

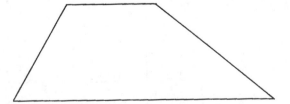

From *Helping Children with Mathematics, Grades 3-5*, published by GoodYearBooks. Copyright © 1996 James Riley, Marge Eberts, and Peggy Gisler.

A trapezoid can be changed into a parallelogram. To do this, have your child draw two same-sized trapezoids using a ruler. Cut one of the trapezoids into two pieces along a line that is halfway between the two parallel bases. Rotate the top piece and join it to the bottom piece to form a parallelogram as shown below. Tape or glue the newly formed parallelogram onto a piece of paper.

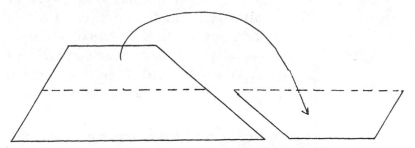

Have your child measure the length of the base and the altitude of the newly formed parallelogram. Have her determine the area of this parallelogram.

Now, have your child measure the dimensions of the uncut trapezoid. The two parallel sides of a trapezoid are called Base 1 and Base 2. The distance between the two parallel lines is called the altitude of the trapezoid. Have her determine the area of the trapezoid by multiplying 1/2 times the altitude times the sum of Base 1 + Base 2.

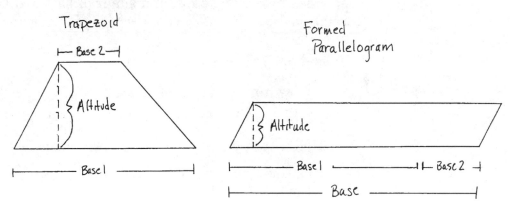

Point out to your child that since the parallelogram was made from the trapezoid, then their areas are the same. Have your child confirm this by comparing the area of the formed parallelogram with the area of the trapezoid.

Also, the length of the altitude of the formed parallelogram is one-half the length of the altitude of the trapezoid. The formula for the area of a trapezoid is the formula for a parallelogram with one-half the altitude.

Parallelogram:	Area = Base x Altitude
Trapezoid:	Area = 1/2 x Altitude x (Base 1 + Base 2)

From *Helping Children with Mathematics, Grades 3–5*, published by GoodYearBooks. Copyright © 1996 James Riley, Marge Eberts, and Peggy Gisler.

Volume Measurement

The measurement of a container's volume is the number of unit measures needed to fill the container. For example, how many cups of water are needed to fill a quart container? The activity in this section will familiarize your child with some of the unit measures used to determine volume. In school, students are generally shown a conversion table and are required to change units using the table. Children understand these relationships better if they learn them through actual measuring activities.

Volume Measurement Activity 1

In the Kitchen

(age 8 and older)

▼

Materials

A quart container
Measuring cups
Measuring spoons
Sugar or salt

Procedure

In this activity your child will determine the relationship between common kitchen measures. Have her use the measuring spoons, measuring cups, and sugar or salt to discover the following relationships by answering a series of questions.

Teaspoon, Tablespoon, and Cup

1. How many teaspoons are in a cup?

2. How many tablespoons are in a cup?

3. How many teaspoons are in a tablespoon?

4. Can you answer question 3 based upon your answers to questions 1 and 2?

Cup, Pint, and Quart

1. How many cups are in a pint?

2. How many cups are in a quart?

3. How many pints are in a quart?

4. Can you answer question 3 based upon your answers to questions 1 and 2?

Explore other measurement relationships with your child in the same manner as above. See how gallons are related to cups, pints, and quarts. Notice how all of the measuring spoons in your set are related to each other.

From *Helping Children with Mathematics, Grades 3–5*, published by GoodYearBooks. Copyright © 1996 James Riley, Marge Eberts, and Peggy Gisler.

Time Measurement

In his book *The Child's Concept of Time*, famous child psychologist Jean Piaget argues convincingly that children are not capable of dealing with the measure of time until about the age of eight. It is in third, fourth, and fifth grades that children refine their "time telling" skills until most become proficient time tellers by sixth grade. The activities in this section are designed to help children read clocks to the hour and then to five-minute intervals.

Time Measurement Activity 1

Call Time Out

(age 8 and older)

From *Helping Children with Mathematics, Grades 3–5*, published by GoodYearBooks. Copyright © 1996 James Riley, Marge

Materials

A big clock

Small write-on
 stickers

Wristwatch

▼

Procedure

Clocks are confusing instruments. The short hand sometimes points to the hour. Mostly it points between the hours. The long hand points to minutes. But there are no minutes on the clock face, only hours. To help your child straighten all of this out, fix up a clock with a fairly large face in this special way.

Take off the face of the clock, and paint the minute hand green. Place small stickers next to the hour numerals on the clock face. Write the number of minutes of the hour on these stickers in the same color you painted the minute hand. The clock face should look like this.

Before teaching your child how to read the minute hand, make sure she knows how to handle the hours. Have her use language like "it's almost four o'clock," "four o'clock," a little after four o'clock, and "halfway between four o'clock and five o'clock" to describe the hour. Move the hour hand on the clock to help her practice different times.

The next step is to teach her how to tell time at five-minute intervals. Have her go around the clock counting by fives. Then move the minute hand to different five-minute intervals for more practice. Keep the clock in a visible spot, and ask your child to tell the time frequently to the closest five-minute interval.

Further Work

Extend your child's time telling capabilities by having her count the minutes between different five-minute intervals. Then ask her to tell you the time throughout the day for more practice.

If your child does not have a wristwatch with a face, buy her one. Your child should not have a digital watch. When we use a watch, we are interested in the relation of the present time to a time in the future or past. It is 7:15 A.M., and the bus leaves at 7:35 A.M. How much time do we have? With a digital watch, the answer requires an arithmetic operation. A traditional watch requires a geometric solution. Children can relate time in a geometric sense more easily than in an arithmetic sense.

Let your child be responsible for managing her own time. She can start her homework at a certain time, be home for dinner at 6 o'clock, and go to bed at the prescribed time.

From *Helping Children with Mathematics, Grades 3–5*, published by GoodYearBooks. Copyright © 1996 James Riley, Marge Eberts, and Peggy Gisler.

Appendix

Materials

The materials in this appendix and in this book's insert are to be used with the following activities:

Block Cards	Region I Activity 2
	Region II Activities 1, 2
	Region III Activity 1
Tic-Tac Game Boards	Region I Activity 4
Advanced Tic-Tac Game Boards	All Regions Activity 1
Blank Multiplication Table	All Regions Activity 2
Multipaths Playing Board	All Regions Activity 3
Divingo Game Sheet	Division Activity 3
Cross Out Game Sheet	Division Activity 4
Fraction Pieces	Fraction Concept Activity 1
Tessellation Shapes	A Different Geometry Activity 2
Tessellations	A Different Geometry Activity 3
Regular Solids	Solid Geometry Activity 1

When you need these materials for an activity, remove the appropriate page or pages from the book. Make a photocopy of the materials. For some of the materials glue them onto cardboard to make them more durable. For even greater durability, laminate those materials. Keep prepared materials in separate envelopes in a box so they are always ready to be used.

Block Cards

Make two sets of block cards. Color the squares red, green, blue, and yellow.

red

red

green

green

blue

blue

yellow

yellow

Divingo Game Sheets

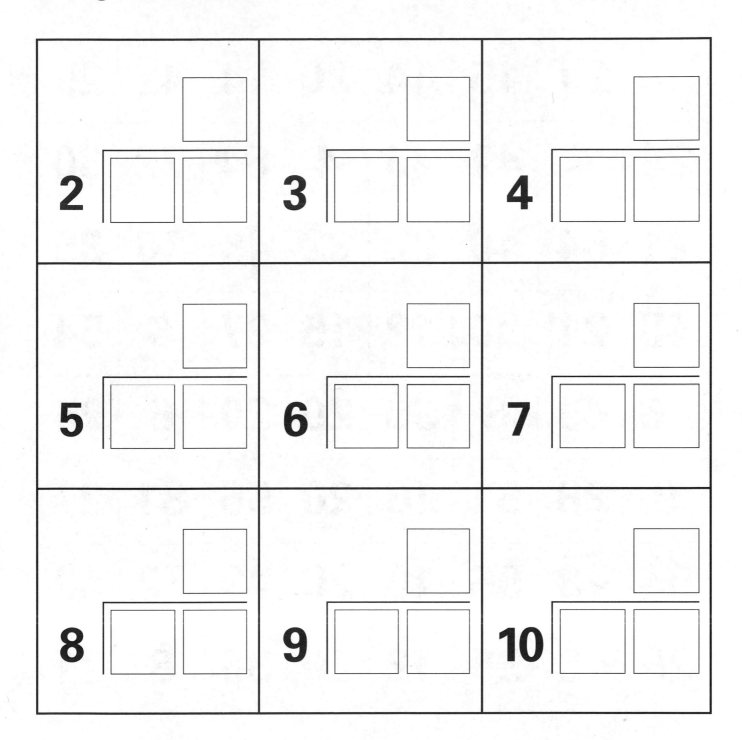

Cross Out Game Sheets

18	21	15	14	20	14	42	25
24	4	42	45	4	64	72	30
21	64	40	32	32	45	10	35
48	21	30	12	15	27	6	54
16	49	8	36	20	20	6	24
9	28	81	18	20	56	81	27
54	48	56	10	20	49	72	40
25	45	35	12	20	36	8	21

Fraction Pieces

One											

| $\dfrac{1}{2}$ | | | | | | $\dfrac{1}{2}$ | | | | | |

| $\dfrac{1}{3}$ | | | | $\dfrac{1}{3}$ | | | | $\dfrac{1}{3}$ | | | |

| $\dfrac{1}{4}$ | | | $\dfrac{1}{4}$ | | | $\dfrac{1}{4}$ | | | $\dfrac{1}{4}$ | | |

| $\dfrac{1}{5}$ | | $\dfrac{1}{5}$ | | $\dfrac{1}{5}$ | | $\dfrac{1}{5}$ | | | $\dfrac{1}{5}$ | | |

| $\dfrac{1}{6}$ | | $\dfrac{1}{6}$ | | $\dfrac{1}{6}$ | | $\dfrac{1}{6}$ | | $\dfrac{1}{6}$ | | $\dfrac{1}{6}$ | |

| $\dfrac{1}{8}$ | $\dfrac{1}{8}$ | $\dfrac{1}{8}$ | $\dfrac{1}{8}$ | $\dfrac{1}{8}$ | $\dfrac{1}{8}$ | $\dfrac{1}{8}$ | $\dfrac{1}{8}$ | | | | |

| $\dfrac{1}{9}$ | $\dfrac{1}{9}$ | $\dfrac{1}{9}$ | $\dfrac{1}{9}$ | $\dfrac{1}{9}$ | $\dfrac{1}{9}$ | $\dfrac{1}{9}$ | $\dfrac{1}{9}$ | $\dfrac{1}{9}$ | | | |

| $\dfrac{1}{10}$ | $\dfrac{1}{10}$ | $\dfrac{1}{10}$ | $\dfrac{1}{10}$ | $\dfrac{1}{10}$ | $\dfrac{1}{10}$ | $\dfrac{1}{10}$ | $\dfrac{1}{10}$ | $\dfrac{1}{10}$ | $\dfrac{1}{10}$ | | |

| $\dfrac{1}{12}$ | $\dfrac{1}{12}$ | $\dfrac{1}{12}$ | $\dfrac{1}{12}$ | $\dfrac{1}{12}$ | $\dfrac{1}{12}$ | $\dfrac{1}{12}$ | $\dfrac{1}{12}$ | $\dfrac{1}{12}$ | $\dfrac{1}{12}$ | $\dfrac{1}{12}$ | $\dfrac{1}{12}$ |

Tessellation Shapes

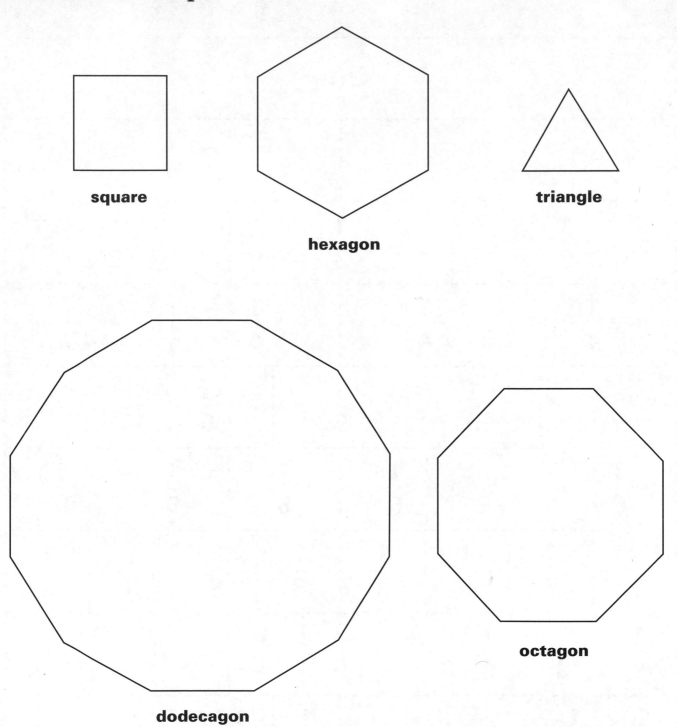

square

hexagon

triangle

dodecagon

octagon

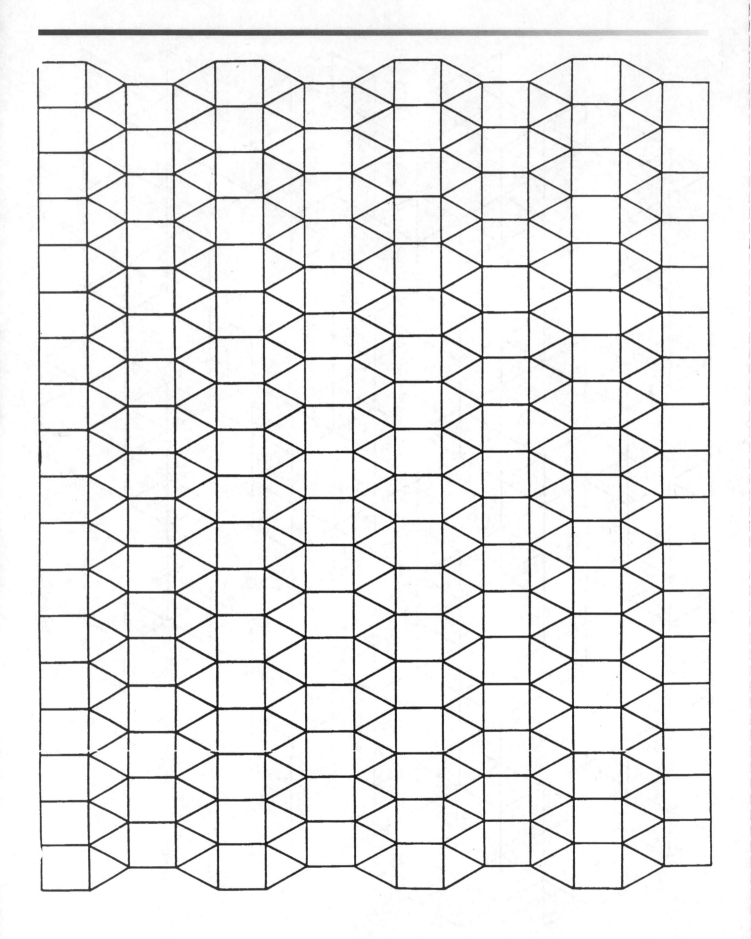

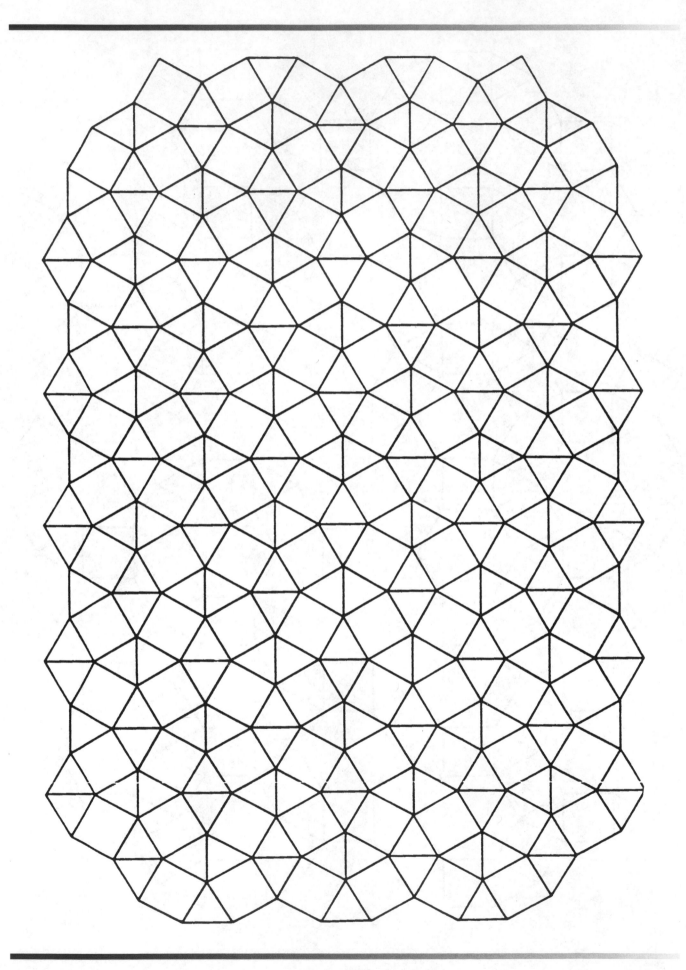

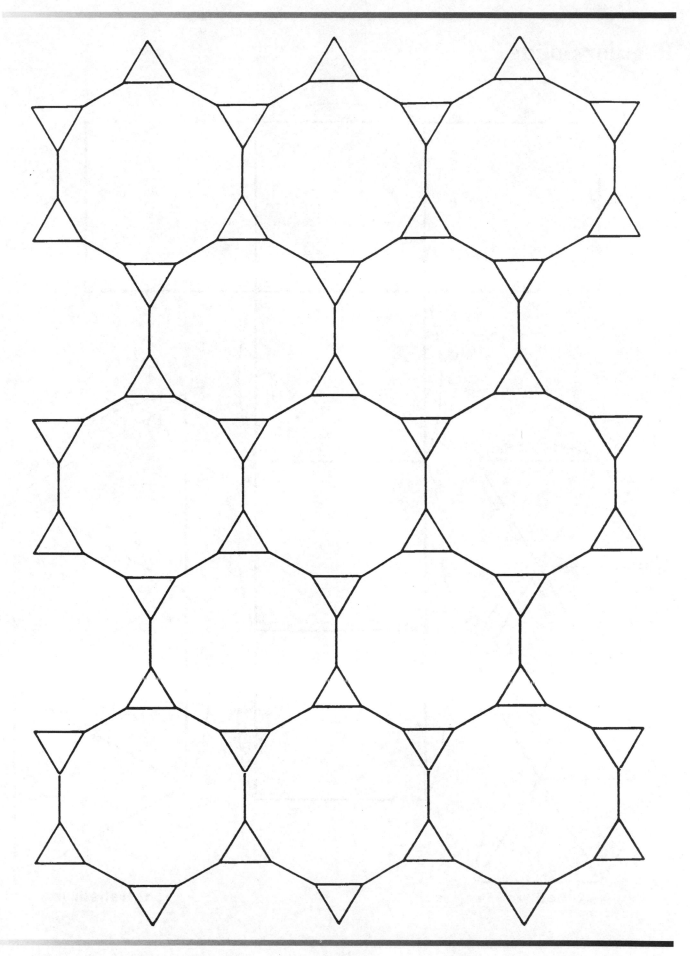

Regular Solids

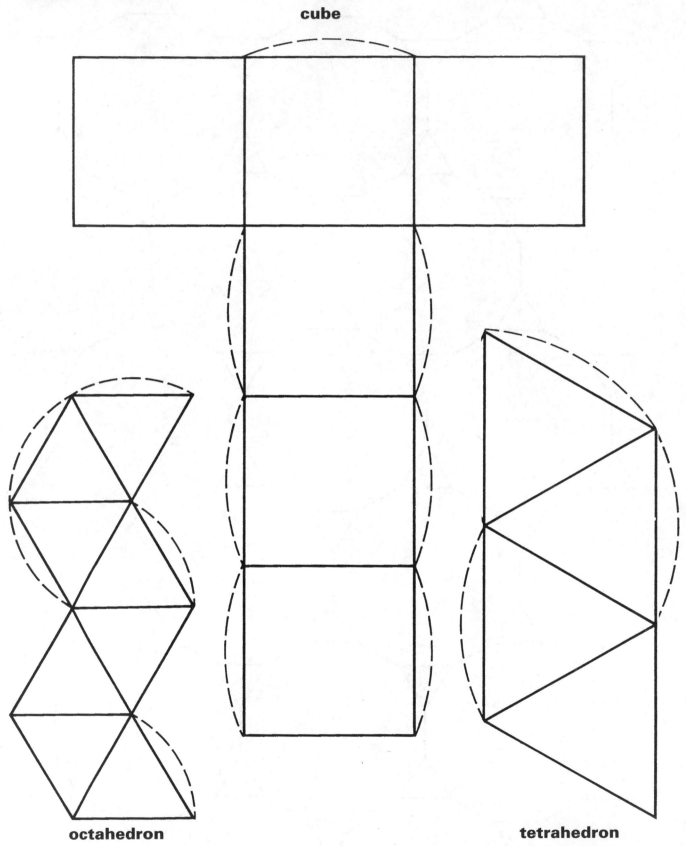

cube

octahedron

tetrahedron

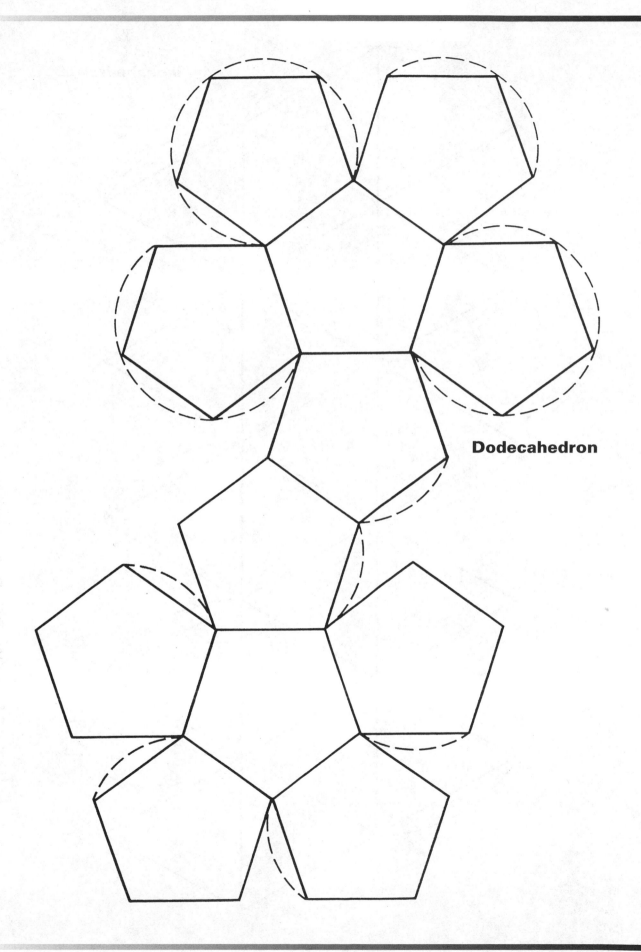

Dodecahedron

Icosahedron